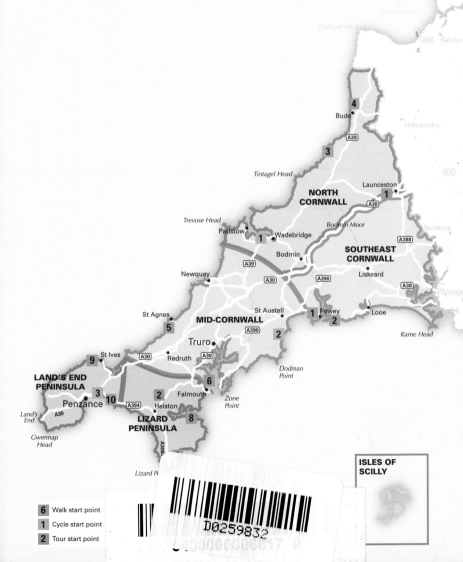

Latchet
Island

Iltracombe

Hartland Point

A39

Bideford

Bude

A39

Holsworthy

A30

Launceston

Tintagel Head

NORTH
CORNWALL

A30

Bodmin Moor

Tavistock

A388

Trevose Head

Padstow

Wadebridge

SOUTHEAST
CORNWALL

A390

Liskeard

A38

Plymouth

Bodmin

A39

Newquay

St Agnes

A30

St Austell

Fowey

Looe

A390

MID-CORNWALL

Rame Head

A390

Truro

Dodman
Point

St Ives

A30

Redruth

A39

LAND'S END
PENINSULA

Zone
Point

Penzance

Falmouth

Land's
End

A30

Helston

LIZARD
PENINSULA

A394

Gwennap
Head

A308

Lizard P

ISLES OF
SCILLY

6 Walk start point

1 Cycle start point

2 Tour start point

D0259832

LEISURE GUIDE

AA

Cornwall

Author: Des Hannigan
Verifier: David Hancock
Managing Editor: David Popey
Project Management: Bookwork Creative Associates Ltd
Designers: Liz Baldin of Bookwork and Andrew Milne
Picture Library Manager: Ian Little
Picture Research: Liz Allen and Vivien Little
Cartography provided by the Mapping Services Department of AA Publishing
Copy-editors: Marilynne Lanng of Bookwork and Pamela Stagg
Internal Repro and Image Manipulation: Marion Morris and Neil Smith
Production: Rachel Davis

Produced by AA Publishing
© AA Media Limited 2007
Reprinted 2007, 2008
Updated and revised 2010

Published by AA Publishing (a trading name of AA Media Limited, whose registered office is Fanum House, Basing View, Basingstoke, Hampshire RG21 4EA; registered number 06112600).

ISBN 978-0-7495-6684-5
ISBN 978-0-7495-6697-5 (SS)

A CIP catalogue record for this book is available from the British Library.

The contents of this book are believed correct at the time of printing. Nevertheless, the publishers cannot be held responsible for any errors or omissions or for changes in the details given in this book or for the consequences of any reliance on the information it provides. This does not affect your statutory rights. We have tried to ensure accuracy in this book, but things do change and we would be grateful if readers would advise us of any inaccuracies they may encounter.

We have taken all reasonable steps to ensure that the walks and cycle rides in this book are safe and achievable by people with a realistic level of fitness. However, all outdoor activities involve a degree of risk and the publishers accept no responsibility for any injuries caused to readers while following these walks and cycle rides. For advice on walking and cycling in safety, see pages 16–17.

Some of the walks and cycle routes may appear

Visit AA Publishing at theAA.com/shop

Printed and bound in China by C&C

A04393

CONTENTS

BUDE

Welcome to...
Cornwall

INTRODUCTION

Cornwall's long, dwindling peninsula draws you westwards from the River Tamar to the towering granite cliffs at Land's End, where England finally gives way to the Atlantic. Nowhere are you more than 20 miles (32km) from the county's dramatic, yet contrasting coastline. The rugged north is a land of mystery and legend and Atlantic-lashed cliffs, while the south is more passive, green and intimate, with deep bays and peaceful coves between bold promontories. Inland, you will find the old tin-mining districts, the lonely, granite heights of Bodmin Moor, the larger towns of rural Cornwall, and a maze of quiet lanes and tranquil villages to explore.

Cornwall has more sandy beaches and coastline than almost anywhere else in Britain. There are 268 miles (431km) of dramatic coastal path to discover – across cliff-tops, past magnificent, golden beaches and through picturesque fishing villages. Surfing reigns supreme in the north on a series of beaches between Bude and Newquay. This is where you will also find superb family beaches with wide sweeps of golden sand.

With more than 50 miles (80km) of heritage coastline, Bronze Age stone circles, cliff castles and a rich industrial heritage, Cornwall has a fascinating history. Geology and mining come to life at Geevor and Poldark mines with underground tours, while a stroll along the coastal path near Land's End and St Agnes reveals old engine houses peering out to sea from high cliff-tops. For an insight into Cornwall's rich maritime heritage visit the superb National Maritime Museum Cornwall at Falmouth.

Beyond Cornwall's spectacular Eden Project, the huge domes and the crowds, and the restored Lost Gardens of Heligan, you will find more than 70 gardens scattered across the county, celebrating the kind climate.

The arts scene is as diverse as the scenery. Don't miss Tate St Ives and Penlee House Gallery in Penzance, and take in a magical open-air play at the Minack Theatre, a spectacular natural amphitheatre carved into the towering cliffs above Porthcurno.

Beyond Land's End, 30 miles (48km) offshore, are the Isles of Scilly, an immaculate archipelago that basks in the warmth of the Gulf Stream, with golden, crowd-free beaches, crystal-clear seas, quiet green corners inland, lush subtropical gardens and an altogether slower pace of life than you will find on mainland Cornwall.

Lundy Island

Ilfracombe

Hartland Point

A39 Bideford

Holsworthy

4
Bude

A39

3

A30

Tintagel Head

Launceston

1

A30

Tavistock

NORTH CORNWALL

Bodmin Moor

A388

Trevose Head

Padstow

1

Wadebridge

Bodmin

SOUTHEAST CORNWALL

A39

Newquay

A30

A390

Liskeard

A38

Plymou

St Agnes

5

St Austell

1 Fowey

2

Looe

MID-CORNWALL

A390

2

Truro

Rame Head

St Ives

9

A30

Redruth

A39

Dodman Point

LAND'S END PENINSULA

3

10

A394

6

Falmouth

Zone Point

Penzance

Helston

2

Land's End

A30

8

Gwennap Head

LIZARD PENINSULA

A3083

7

Lizard Point

ISLES OF SCILLY

6 Walk start point

1 Cycle start point

2 Tour start point

Essential Sights

Cornwall is a county of dramatic contrasts: the Isles of Scilly, Land's End and the north Cornish coast belong to the bracing Atlantic, while the Lizard Peninsula and south Cornwall have gentler more intimate climates. The granite spine of central Cornwall runs from the old tin-mining district of Land's End to the lonely heights of Bodmin Moor, while on either side lies secluded countryside dotted with tiny villages and a host of diverse holiday attractions.

1 Tate St Ives
This wonderful purpose-built showcase for contemporary art displays works by leading artists of the St Ives School.

2 The Lost Gardens of Heligan
The Giant's Head is part of these remarkable gardens, which were restored during the early 1990s after being abandoned for more than 80 years.

3 Cotehele
The well-preserved and charming manor house and gardens of Cotehele give a fascinating insight into how wealthy people lived in Tudor Cornwall.

4 Eden Project
An orange tree flourishes in the Warm Temperate Biome, which emulates the natural landscapes of the Mediterranean, South Africa and California.

5 Tintagel
The stone ramparts of Tintagel Castle defend a spectacular headland overlooking the wild north Cornish coast.

6 Golitha Falls
The River Fowey flows through oak and beech woodland in a steep-sided valley gorge at this beauty spot on the southern edge of Bodmin Moor.

7 Chysauster Ancient Village

The unique Celtic settlement of Chysauster consists of stone-walled homesteads, all with a central courtyard with small rooms leading off. The village, approached via a steep slope, was originally occupied over more than 2,000 years ago.

8 Helford Estuary

Whitewashed cottages and small craft at Gwithian, situated on the peaceful tree-lined tidal creeks of the Helford Estuary.

9 Fistral Beach, Newquay

Golden Fistral Beach, seen here at low tide at sunset when the surfers have departed, hosts world-class surfing championships during the summer months. It is just one of a number of beaches in Newquay.

10 Millook, Widemouth Bay

Fine narrow footpaths, part of the South West Coast Path, thread the rugged landscape at Millook, just south of Bude. In spring the paths are dotted with pink clumps of sea thrift.

11 St Agnes

A stepped terrace of picturesque stone-built cottages, called Stippy Stappy, in the unassuming coastal village of St Agnes.

9

10

11

Day One

Cornwall and the Scilly Isles have so much to offer visitors – magnificent coastal walks, watersports, fine eating – it can be difficult to fit it all in, especially on a weekend break or a long weekend. These four pages offer a loosely planned itinerary designed to ensure that you make the most of your time and see and enjoy the very best the area has to offer.

Friday Night

Stay in St Ives at The Garrack, a small hotel situated high above the town in secluded surroundings. Here you can enjoy views of the spectacular coastal scenery, including Porthmeor Beach, along with the welcoming atmosphere and wonderful food.

Wander around the harbour area at St Ives in the evening.

Saturday Morning

Stroll through attractive Fore Street, and on along the narrow, cobbled streets of St Ives with their numerous galleries and craft workshops. Visit the Tate St Ives and the Barbara Hepworth Gallery and Sculpture Garden.

St Ives' magnificent golden beaches are an alternative attraction when the weather is fine.

Leave St Ives on the B3306 north coast road, via Zennor and Gurnard's Head, through the glorious scenery of the Land's End Peninsula. Just before Morvah, at Trevowhan, turn left to visit the remains of a prehistoric burial chamber at Lanyon Quoit.

Alternatively, remain on the B3306 and continue to Land's End where there are stunning views, exhibitions and wet weather attractions.

Saturday Lunch

Head for Marazion via the A30 and the A394, where a good place for lunch, in summer, is the Mount Haven Hotel at the eastern end of the town. There are splendid views out across Mount's Bay and to St Michael's Mount (right).

Saturday Afternoon

Reach St Michael's Mount, either on foot across the cobbled causeway or by ferry in summer if the tide is in. The Mount is in the care of the National Trust and both house and gardens are delightful. For children, the world of castles and cannons in such a wonderful maritime setting is irresistible.

Take the A394 to Helston and on through Gweek to Mawnan Smith. This is Cornwall's other landscape, a world of magical wooded creeks and quiet lanes, a delightful contrast to the rugged seascapes of St Ives and the wild moorland of the Land's End Peninsula.

Saturday Night

Stay at the Budock Vean Hotel on the banks of the River Helford near Mawnan Smith. Set amidst beautiful gardens and parkland with a private foreshore to the Helford, the hotel includes a golf course among its leisure facilities.

ST MICHAEL'S MOUNT

Day Two

Your second and final day offers a choice of expeditions, on foot, through the Helford area, followed by a visit to one of Cornwall's loveliest gardens, Glendurgan. If the weather is bad, Falmouth, only a short distance away, has numerous wet-weather attractions.

Sunday Morning

If it is wet, drive north to Falmouth and visit the National Maritime Museum Cornwall, which transports visitors into the world of small boats and Cornish maritime history. With entertaining interactive displays. The museum also has a Tidal Zone where you can take advantage of a natural underwater view of the harbour.

The best way to enjoy the beauties of the Helford area is on foot. The northern shore of the estuary, and its adjoining coastline, provides splendid walking.

Alternatively, a ferry trip from Helford Passage takes you to Helford village. From here you can enjoy an easy walk to Frenchman's Creek.

Helford can also be reached by a short drive round the end of the Helford River. The route passes through Gweek where a visit to the Seal Sanctuary will delight children and adults alike.

Sunday Lunch

For lunch, if you decide on a walk round the Mawnan Smith coast, then it might be best to take a picnic. If you cross to Helford, then try the 17th-century Shipwright Arms. This friendly pub, in a delightful riverside setting, provides a good selection of tasty meals.

Sunday Afternoon

Visit the National Trust's Glendurgan Garden, a valley garden of great beauty created in the 1820s. Children will love the laurel maze, which dates from 1833. The adjacent Trebah Garden, which lies in a steep-sided valley, is also delightful. This sub-tropical paradise is home to a large collection of rare and exotic plants. There are several paths through the garden that lead down to a secluded beach on the Helford River.

Don't forget to make time for a delicious cream tea to round off your weekend tour.

Route facts

MINIMUM TIME The time stated for completing each route is the estimated minimum time that a reasonably fit family group of walkers or cyclists would take to complete the circuit. This does not allow for rest or refreshment stops.

OS MAP Each route is shown on a map. However, some detail is lost because of the restrictions imposed by scale, so for this reason, we recommend that you use the maps in conjunction with a more detailed Ordnance Survey map. The relevant map for each walk or cycle ride is listed.

START This indicates the start location and parking area. This is a six-figure grid reference prefixed by two letters showing which 62.5-mile (100km) square of the National Grid it refers to. You'll find more information on grid references on most Ordnance Survey maps.

CYCLE HIRE We list, within reason, the nearest cycle hire shop/centre.

❶ Here we highlight any potential difficulties or dangers along the cycle ride or walk. If a particular route is suitable for older, fitter children we say so here. Also, we give guidelines of a route's suitability for younger children, for example the symbol 8+ indicates that the route can probably be attempted by children aged 8 years and above.

Walks & Cycle Rides

Each walk and cycle ride has a panel giving information for the walker and cyclist, including the distance, terrain, nature of the paths, and where to park your car.

WALKING

All of the walks are suitable for families, but less experienced family groups, especially those with younger children, should try the shorter walks. Route finding is usually straightforward, but the maps are for guidance only and we recommend that you always take the relevant Ordnance Survey map with you.

Risks

Although each walk has been researched with a view to minimising any risks, no walk in the countryside can be considered to be completely free from risk. Walking in the outdoors will always require a degree of common sense and judgement to ensure that it is as safe as possible, especially for young children.
• Be particularly careful on cliff paths and in upland terrain, where the consequences of a slip can be serious.
• Remember to check tidal conditions before walking on the seashore.
• Some sections of route are by, or cross, busy roads.

Remember traffic is a danger even on minor country lanes.
• Be careful around farmyard machinery and livestock.
• Be prepared for the consequences of changes in the weather and check the forecast before you set out.
• Ensure the whole family is properly equipped, wearing suitable clothing and a good pair of boots or sturdy walking shoes. Take waterproof clothing with you and a torch if you are walking in the winter months.
• Remember the weather can change quickly at any time of the year, and in moorland and heathland areas, mist and fog can make route-finding much harder. In summer, take account of the heat and sun by wearing a hat, sunscreen and carrying enough water.
• On walks away from centres of population you should carry a mobile phone, whistle and, if possible, a survival bag. If you do have an accident requiring emergency services, make a note of your position as accurately as possible and dial 999 (112 on a mobile).

CYCLING

In devising the cycle rides in this guide, every effort has been made to use designated cycle paths, or to link them with quiet country lanes and waymarked byways and bridleways. In a few cases, some fairly busy B-roads have been used to join up with quieter routes.

Rules of the road

• Ride in single file on narrow and busy roads.

• Be alert, look and listen for traffic, especially on narrow lanes and blind bends and be extra careful when descending steep hills, as loose gravel or a poor road surface can lead to an accident.

• In wet weather make sure that you keep an appropriate distance between you and other riders.

• Make sure you indicate your intentions clearly.

• Brush up on *The Highway Code* before venturing out onto the road.

Off-road safety code of conduct

• Only ride where you know it is legal to do so. Cyclists are not allowed to cycle on public footpaths (yellow waymarkers). The only 'rights of way' open to cyclists are bridleways (blue markers) and unsurfaced tracks, known as byways, which are open to all traffic and waymarked in red.

• Canal tow paths: you need a permit to cycle on some stretches of tow path (www.waterscape.com). Remember that access paths can be steep and slippery so always push your bike under low bridges and by locks.

• Always yield to walkers and horses, giving adequate warning of your approach.

• Don't expect to cycle at high speeds.

• Keep to the main trail to avoid any unnecessary erosion to the area beside the trail and to prevent skidding, especially in wet weather conditions.

• Remember to follow the Country Code.

Preparing your bicycle

Check the wheels, tyres, brakes and cables. Lubricate hubs, pedals, gear mechanisms and cables. Make sure you have a pump, a bell, a rear rack to carry panniers and a set of lights.

Equipment

• A cycling helmet provides essential protection.

• Make sure you are visible to other road users, by wearing light-coloured or luminous clothing in daylight and sashes or reflective strips in failing light and darkness.

• Take extra clothes with you, depending on the season, and a wind/waterproof jacket.

• Carry a basic tool kit, a pump, a strong lock and a first aid kit.

• Always carry enough water for your outing.

Walk Map Legend

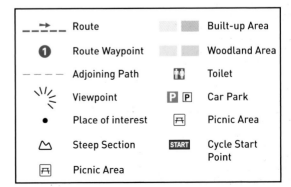

⇢	Route		Built-up Area
❶	Route Waypoint		Woodland Area
– – –	Adjoining Path	🚻	Toilet
☀	Viewpoint	P P	Car Park
•	Place of interest	🏠	Picnic Area
⌂	Steep Section	START	Cycle Start Point
🏠	Picnic Area		

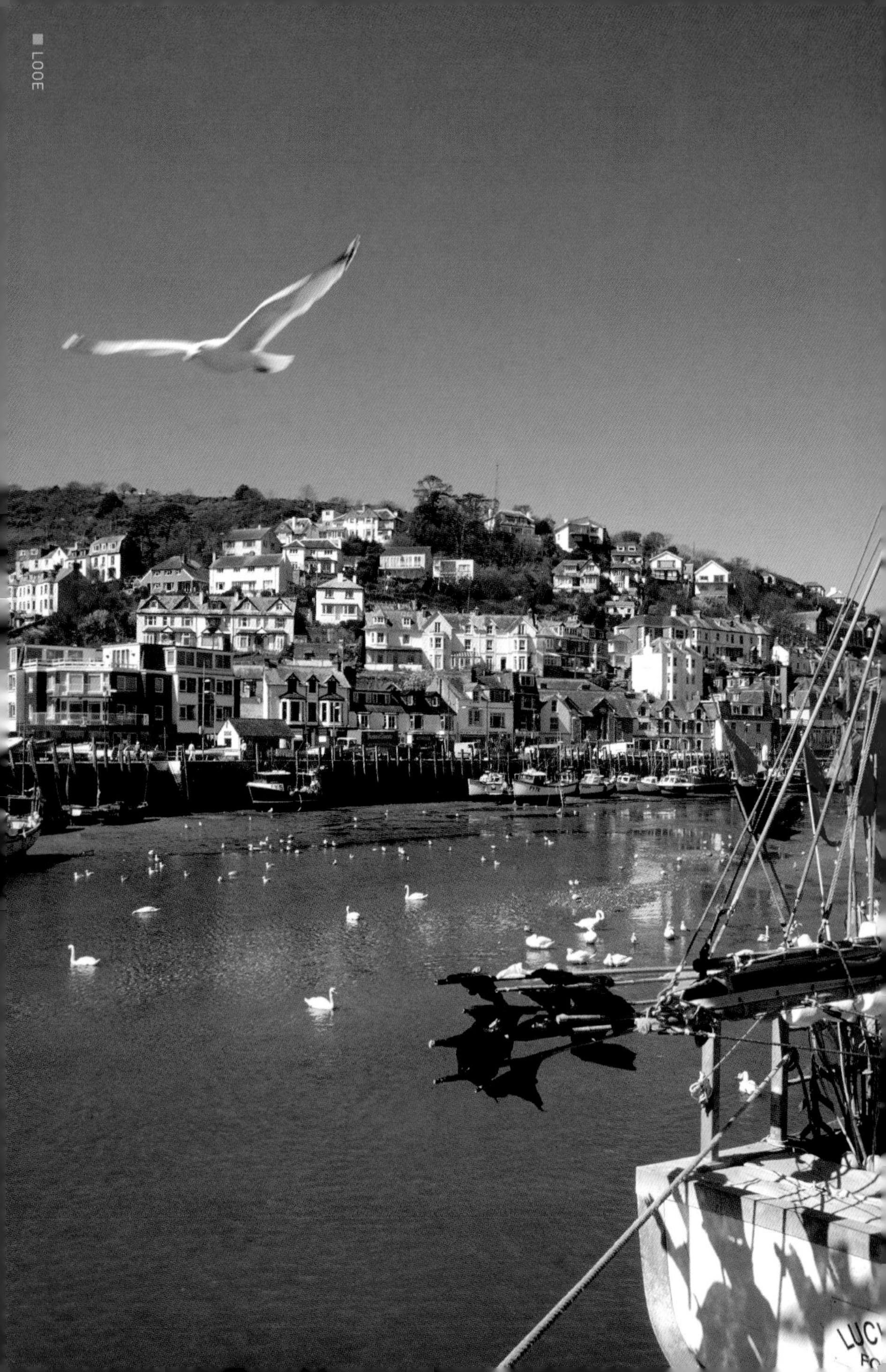

Southeast Cornwall

Southeast Cornwall is where singing rivers run south from the high ground of Bodmin Moor through woods and well-farmed fields to reach one of the loveliest coastlines in England. It is a coast that begins within sight of Plymouth at the peaceful Rame Peninsula, from where it runs west past spacious beaches to the port of Looe and the fishing village of Polperro. Further west the coastline traces its intricate way in and out of tiny coves and around handsome headlands as far as Fowey's graceful estuary and town. Between the granite country of the high moor and the coast are the bustling market towns of Liskeard and Lostwithiel and the quiet villages of an older Cornwall.

2 Walk start point

POLPERRO

BODMIN MOOR

Unmissable attractions

Sunny south Cornwall invites relaxation, but there's enough adventure here to tempt even the most devoted beach addict. The secluded and beautiful Roseland Peninsula at the mouth of Falmouth Bay is where it all starts. From here to the distant Rame Peninsula on the shores of Plymouth Sound lies one of the loveliest coastlines in Britain, a long meandering water margin that traces its intricate way in and out of tiny coves, past quiet beaches and fascinating towns and villages, such as Fowey and Looe. The coast is easily accessible, yet the outside world seems firmly shut out by a tangle of shady woods, coastal hills and secluded valleys.

1 Golitha Falls
The River Fowey enters a whitewater section of rapids as it makes its way through a steep, wooded valley gorge. The falls are best appreciated after a period of heavy rain.

2 Hurlers Stone Circles
These three granite stone circles on Bodmin Moor date from the Bronze Age. According to local tradition they are men turned into stone.

3 Cawsand
Situated on the Rame Peninsula, the unspoiled fishing village of Cawsand is an ideal place to sit and relax away from the bustle and the crowds.

4 Lanhydrock
In the care of the National Trust, Lanhydrock is part Jacobean and part Victorian. This imposing house, which gives a vivid picture of life in Victorian times, is set in magnificent grounds with colourful formal gardens. The higher garden, behind the house, is famed for its magnolias and rhododendrons.

5 Talland Bay
Waves break on the bay's small sandy beach, which is flanked by flat beds of rock beneath the striking headland. It was used as a smuggling base during the 17th and early 18th centuries.

ANTONY HOUSE   MAP REF SX4256

Antony House, home of the Carew family for generations, is now cared for by the National Trust and stands in more than 100 acres (40ha) of woodland garden on the grassy banks of the Lynher River near Torpoint. The original Tudor house was pulled down in the early part of the 18th century and replaced by the finest Georgian house in Cornwall, perfectly proportioned with fine granite stonework facings of Pentewan stone and elegant colonnaded wings of red brick.

CALSTOCK   MAP REF SX4368

Calstock is Cornish, but its position is deceptive. It stands within a final enclave of Cornwall on the deep meanders of the River Tamar (the county boundary) that protrudes into Devon.

Calstock has been an important River Tamar quay since the Saxons arrived in Cornwall. For many centuries, sand and lime carried upriver on Tamar barges were used for improving the soil of surrounding farms. Tin and copper, and quarried granite from nearby Kit Hill, were transported back to Plymouth and at Calstock there was shipbuilding, and paper- and brick-making. Until the railway came to the Tamar Valley, full-masted schooners, steam-powered coasters, barges and paddle steamers all berthed at Calstock's quay.

Later, in the 20th century, market gardening in the surrounding area was a thriving business, but Calstock's great industrial days are long gone, leaving a rich heritage amidst the loveliness of the Tamar countryside. Calstock's great glory is its viaduct – built in 1906 with manufactured blocks, it is a triumph of good design and engineering. Today, the railway still links Calstock to the outer world, but it remains a river settlement and passenger boats from Plymouth still come upriver to tie up at Calstock, where pubs and restaurants, shops and galleries add to the attractions.

West of Calstock is Cotehele (National Trust), a Tudor house of great beauty that lies in deep woods in elegant seclusion. The Tudor style of the house has been preserved virtually intact thanks to the fact that in 1533 the owner, Richard Edgcumbe, built Mount Edgcumbe House on Plymouth Sound and made that the family seat. Cotehele then became a second home. Even the furnishings at Cotehele have a rare antiquity, with intricate tapestries of Flemish design and beautifully decorated furniture. There is no electric light at Cotehele, so avoid visiting the house on a dull day.

■ Visit

KIT HILL

The magnificent granite dome of Kit Hill rises to just over 1,000 feet (305m) above the town of Callington, about 4 miles (6.4km) northwest of Calstock. It stands in splendid isolation, as if torn between the granite masses of Bodmin Moor to the west and Dartmoor to the east. For centuries Kit Hill was quarried for stone and delved into for tin, copper, zinc, lead and even silver, but it is now a country park. The hill is crowned by an 80-foot (24m) chimney stack built in 1858 as part of the engine house of the Kithill Consols mine. There are pathways around the hill, including both a waymarked walking trail and a heritage trail.

CAWSAND & KINGSAND

MAP REF SX4350

The villages of Cawsand and Kingsand lie on the Rame Peninsula within 3 miles (4.8km) of Plymouth; but because the high ground of Mount Edgcumbe lies between, there is no awareness of a large city and port being so close. The two villages, which now merge, were once divided by the old Devon–Cornwall border between Saxon England and the Celtic West – look for the sign on Garrett Street. The Saxons took control of both sides of the Tamar, a wise defence against the ever-present threat of Viking raiders.

For many generations those born in Kingsand were recorded as Devon-born, but today Cawsand and Kingsand sit comfortably together in Cornwall. Cawsand has a charming little square above its small beach and from here you can walk along Garrett Street to Kingsand, and past a grand clock tower. Explore the narrow alleyways and flights of steps that sidle to and fro above the rocky shoreline.

Running south from Cawsand is a level walk that leads along part of a Victorian drive, built by the Earl of Edgcumbe. Wealthy landowners of the 18th and 19th centuries often built such driveways through their properties in order to show them off to their full advantage to arriving guests. The way leads through shady woods to Penlee Point, where there is a delightful grotto built against the slope of the headland. From here you can enjoy exhilarating views of the graceful curve of Rame Head as it heads to the west.

■ Visit

MOUNT EDGCUMBE COUNTRY PARK

The original Tudor house at Mount Edgcumbe was destroyed by a bomb during the Second World War, a victim of the massive raids on Plymouth. It was rebuilt during the 1960s to replicate the original and has been handsomely restored. The landscaped park has many engaging features, such as follies, mock temples and Gothic ruins, and exquisite formal gardens. The park's woodland has a network of paths and fallow deer roam among the trees. Nearby is the little river port of Cremyll from where there is a passenger ferry to Plymouth.

EAST BODMIN MOOR

MAP REF SX2574

Cornwall's largest area of high moorland has been bisected by the A30, but the moor falls naturally into contrasting east and west sectors. The eastern side seems less wild and rugged than the undulating hills and rocky ridges of Brown Willy and Rough Tor to the west, while around the remote village of Minions it has all the raw beauty of wild country. The moor has been torn apart in places. The ragged, gaping hole of Cheesewring Quarry above Minions is the result of a moorland industry that was as vigorous as the copper mining that left behind great engine houses at nearby Phoenix United Mine.

Cheesewring's granite was used to build Devonport Dockyard, Birkenhead Docks and part of Copenhagen Harbour and was included in the materials used in the Thames Embankment and Westminster and Tower bridges.

The quarry's name comes from the remarkable formation of layered granite that stands at its western edge, named after its similarity to a cider press used to squeeze the 'cheese' or juice from apples. It is formed by erosion of the weaker horizontal joints in the granite.

Close to the southwestern edge of the quarry is the reconstructed cave dwelling of Daniel Gumb, who was a stone-cutter in the 18th century. He built a much larger original cave dwelling here for himself and his family. Gumb was blessed with considerable intellectual gifts. He was known as 'the Mountain Philosopher' and was said to be well versed in astronomy and mathematics. Gumb's original cave was destroyed when Cheesewring Quarry was extended in the 1870s, but the roof of the present one is part of the original and has on its surface a carving of one of Euclid's theorems. Minions Heritage Centre, in a Cornish engine house, has displays on the history of the landscape

■ Visit

DOZMARY POOL
Atmospheric Dozmary Pool, on the A30, positively boils with myth and legend. The most enduring myth tells the tale of the infamous Jan Tregeagle, a rather nasty piece of work. It's actually a composite character of several generations of the Tregeagles, who were powerful lawyers, magistrates and land stewards between the 16th and 18th centuries, and notorious for their callous brutality and dishonesty. For their dirty deeds, Jan Tregeagle, a disgruntled spirit, is condemned by the devil to impossible tasks, such as baling out Dozmary Pool with a holed shell.

from the Stone Age, through 18th- and 19th-century mining and up until today.

Bodmin Moor is much older than its mining industry. Close to Minions village is a cluster of early Bronze Age (2500–1500BC) monuments including the stone circles of the Hurlers and their adjacent standing stones. Craddock Moor to the west is peppered with burial mounds from the Bronze Age, hut circles of the Iron Age, and medieval field systems. North of Minions is Twelve Men's Moor and the rocky ridges of Kilmar Tor and Bearah Tor. Further north, a broad sweep of moorland runs through marshy ground to Fox Tor and then washes up against the asphalt boundary of the A30. To the west, the River Fowey flows from near Bolventor and Jamaica Inn, through a long, shallow valley. There are reservoirs with the characteristics of natural lakes at Colliford and Siblyback, and where the Fowey turns to the west at Draynes Bridge it pours through deep woods and moss-shrouded boulders at Golitha Falls. North of Minions, the moor drops suddenly into the deeply wooded valley of the River Lynher with peaceful hillside villages, such as North Hill.

FOWEY MAP REF SX1251
Buildings crowd out Fowey's waterfront but there is a wonderful sense of unity within the jumble of narrow streets and there is access to the harbour and quay from various points. Fowey (pronounced 'Foy') was a major port from the earliest times. More than 700 seamen from the town and its surrounding parishes took part in the Siege of Calais in 1346 when

the town supplied 47 vessels compared to London's 25. In return, Fowey was attacked and burned by the French in 1380 and in 1467. It was the Port of Cornwall in every sense and its seamen earned the title 'the Fowey Gallants'. These outstanding sailors were known for their arrogance and contempt for the law, and their energies soon turned to lucrative piracy. When Edward IV took a grip on the port, Fowey turned to equally lucrative, but honest, trade. China clay and the enterprise of the Treffry family brought prosperity, and today ocean-going ships pass upriver to Golant' quays from where clay is still exported.

Fowey draws you in from the long descent of Lostwithiel Street to Trafalgar Square, then on round the Town Quay and Webb Street. The buildings crowd in from all sides and even the dark-stoned Church of St Fimbarrus with its decorated tower seems to overhang. The true face of Fowey is seen from the river or from Polruan on the opposite shore. Tall houses rise sheer from the waterfront, and when night falls in summer the boat-bobbing river is starred with lights. From the bottom of Lostwithiel Street, the Esplanade leads southwest to Readymoney Cove, where a small sandy beach lies below tree-shrouded St Catherine's Point.

St Catherine's Castle crowns the Point; built between 1538 and 1542 as part of the chain of defences set up along the coast by Henry VIII in response to hostility from France and the Holy Roman Empire. The castle can be reached up steep steps from the beach or by a leisurely track.

■ Activity

FERRY EXCURSIONS

A relaxing way to visit Polruan from Fowey is to go by ferry. In summer a passenger ferry leaves from Whitehouse Slip, off the Esplanade (evenings from Town Quay); a winter service runs from Fowey's Town Quay. Take a bike on the ferry and follow the minor road east from Polruan to Lansallos and then on to Polperro, or walk along the coast path to Pencarrow Head and Lansallos. A summer passenger ferry also runs regularly to Mevagissey. Coastal and river cruises also operate from the Town Quay. A car ferry at Caffamill Pill goes to Bodinnick, across the River Fowey.

Driving through Fowey should be avoided at the busiest times. The main car park at the entrance to the town is signed from the A3082. You will find a good mix of shops lining the bustling streets, along with fine galleries, craft and antique shops. Fowey's pubs are full of a sea-going atmosphere and there are several good restaurants. The museum is in the town hall at Trafalgar Square and the Tourist Information Centre is at the far end of Fore Street.

Overlooking the town is Place, the historic home of the Treffry family (not open). The original 15th-century house was rebuilt in Regency Gothic style during the 19th century and it is a delightfully eccentric building.

Tree-shrouded Golant lies 1.5 miles (2.4km) north of Fowey and is reached from the B3269. In this charming village the small but absorbing Church of St Sampson commemorates one of Cornwall's great Celtic saints.

From Fowey to Polkerris

Explore the coast and countryside near Fowey where writer Daphne du Maurier found inspiration for her novels. The walk starts from Readymoney Cove and follows Love Lane that rises over rock slabs into Covington Wood. The route strikes inland along field paths and enclosed tracks. In the valley below Lankelly Farm the path passes through a tunnel and beneath a former carriageway leading to Menabilly House. Beyond Tregaminion Farm and church the western flank of the Gribbin Peninsula is reached where you can divert to Polkerris Cove, the beach and the Rashleigh Inn. Follow the coastal footpath south to Gribbin Head then north to Polridmouth Cove, then St Catherine's Point and a steep descent back to Readymoney Cove.

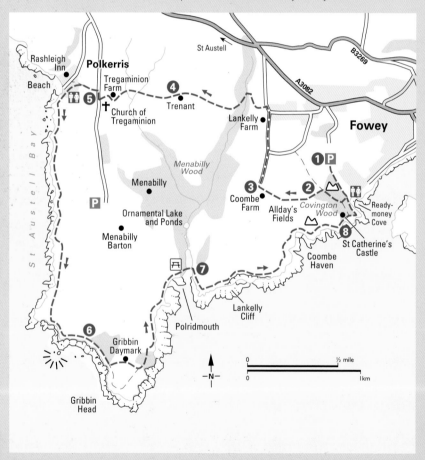

Route Directions

1 From the bottom end of the car park walk down St Catherine's Parade, then turn right towards the inlet of Readymoney Cove. Continue to the end of the road, above the beach and follow the initially rocky Love Lane uphill on the Saints Way. Carry on past the first junction, ignoring the options by a National Trust signpost for 'Covington Woods'.

2 Turn left at the next junction and then climb wooden steps to reach Allday's Fields. Follow the right-hand field-edge. At a field gap follow an obvious grassy track ahead to a lane end at Coombe Farm. Follow the lane ahead.

3 At a road, turn right and continue to Lankelly Farm. Pass a junction on the right and follow Prickly Post Lane for a few paces. Turn off left on to a gravel drive, then keep left and along a narrow fenced-in path.

4 After the barn conversions at Trenant, cross a surfaced lane, then a stile. Keep ahead alongside the field-edge, then follow the path to a kissing gate into a field below Tregaminion Farm. Go up the field to a gate, continue between buildings then turn right, then left, to reach a T-junction with a road by the entrance gate to the little Church of Tregaminion.

5 Turn right and in 100yds (91m) go left into a field. Reach a junction on the edge of some woods. (An enjoyable diversion is to take the right-hand branch to Polkerris with its beach and cove and the Rashleigh Inn.) On the main route, keep left along the field-edge and follow the well-defined coast path for 1.25 miles (2km) to Gribbin Head.

6 Enter the wooded National Trust property of the Gribbin. Keep left at a junction. Go through a gate and cross to the Gribbin Daymark. Go left and down a faint grassy track, then follow the coast path along to Polridmouth.

7 Follow the coast path and at open ground, follow the seaward field-edge. Go steeply in to, and out of, Coombe Hawne. Enter Covington Wood, keep left at the immediate junction, and pass the Rashleigh Mausoleum.

8 Turn right at a junction to reach St Catherine's Castle. Return along the path then

Route facts

DISTANCE/TIME 7.5 miles (12km) 4h

MAP OS Explorer 107 St Austell & Liskeard

START Readymoney Cove car park, reached by continuing on from entrance to Fowey's main car park; grid ref: SX 118511

TRACKS Field paths, rough lanes and coastal footpath; 10 stiles

GETTING TO THE START On the edge of Fowey follow signs for the main car park, then continue (signed) to Readymoney Cove car park.

THE PUB The Rashleigh Inn, Polkerris. Tel: 01726 813991; www.rashleighinnpolkerrris.co.uk

❶ There are some steep ascents and descents on the coast path and paths can be muddy and slippery during wet weather. A walk suited to older, fitter family groups.

go down steps at the first junction on the right. Go down wooden steps to reach Readymoney Beach. Return to the car park via St Catherine's Parade.

GRIBBIN HEAD MAP REF SW0949

Southwest of Fowey, Gribbin Head (National Trust) shoulders out the western sea, preventing it from having too much influence on sheltered Fowey. The headland, always referred to as The Gribbin, is crowned with a bizarre monolith – the 84-foot (25m) Daymark tower painted in barber-shop red and white. The Daymark was erected in 1832 in order to distinguish The Gribbin from St Anthony's Head at the entrance to Falmouth Bay. The two headlands look similar from the seaward approach and sailors regularly mistook The Gribbin for St Anthony's Head, with catastrophic results when they sailed blindly into the shallows of St Austell Bay instead of the deep waters of Falmouth Bay.

Inland of The Gribbin is Menabilly, where Daphne du Maurier made her home and found inspiration for a number of her novels. In the eastern shelter of The Gribbin is Polridmouth Cove, with adjoining beaches and an ornamental lake.

The Gribbin can be reached on foot from a car park at Menabilly Barton, a mile (1.6km) inland. To the west, the tiny Polkerris faces into St Austell Bay. There is a car park halfway down the tree-shaded approach, from where it is just a short walk to the pleasant beach.

LANHYDROCK MAP REF SW0863

Magnificent Lanhydrock lies about 2.5 miles (4km) north of Lostwithiel via the B3268, or can be reached from Bodmin via the A30. It is approached along an avenue of stately beech trees, which leads through the beautiful parkland. On first sight the house gives every impression of being wholly Tudor. In fact, all that remains of the original house, built between 1630 and 1642 for wealthy Truro merchant Sir Richard Robartes, is the gatehouse, entrance porch and north wing. The east wing was removed, and the rest fell victim to a terrible fire in 1881, but the house was rebuilt to match the surviving part.

The interiors are very grand, notably the Long Gallery, and there are lavish furnishings throughout the house. Of all the 50 rooms that are open, visitors tend to find the 'below stairs' sections of most interest, including the kitchen, larders, bakehouse, dairy, cellars and servants' quarters.

Lanhydrock is surrounded by beautiful grounds, with some pleasant rides and paths to stroll along. Adjoining the house are formal gardens with clipped yews and bronze urns, while the higher garden is famed for its magnolias and rhododendrons.

LISKEARD MAP REF SX2564

With Bodmin Moor to the north, and Looe to the south, Liskeard is an ideal holiday centre. Liskeard was a Coinage town from medieval times and Coinage endowed the town with a status and prosperity that encouraged other business; copper mining during the 19th century further increased the town's wealth. When mining declined Liskeard continued to thrive as the focus of road and rail communications throughout east Cornwall and is still the northern terminus of the branch railway that connects with Looe.

Today Liskeard's attractive townscape reflects its prosperous history. The streets, quite narrow in places, are flanked by tall buildings. Fine individual examples include the notable Victorian Webb's Hotel, hip-roofed and stolid, which overlooks the Parade, whilst the Guildhall's Italianate tower dominates Market Street. In Well Lane, off Market Street, is the ancient Pipe Well; the water is now considered unfit to drink and the well is gated. Liskeard's Church of St Martin, the second largest church in Cornwall after St Petroc's at Bodmin, suffered some heavy-handed Victorian restoration and is rather dull because of it. Liskeard is a busy shopping centre, in keeping with its commercial traditions. On market days, the country comes to town bringing a refreshing bustle to the streets.

LOOE MAP REF SX2553

Tourism came early to Looe. It is said that the bathing machine arrived at Looe beach as early as 1800 when war with France sent the leisured classes to southwest England in search of a home-grown alternative to French resorts. But it was the arrival of the railway, that led to the growth of the tourism that sustains Looe today.

The old town of East Looe is a delight. There is something of a French style in its ordered layout and in the way the tall buildings seem to accentuate the narrowness of streets and passageways. The houses, some timber-framed but most of stone, are painted in a variety of colours. The old pilchard-curing cellars by the quay are built from unadorned stone and many of the cottages have an outside stone staircase indicating that the ground floors were used as pilchard processing cellars and net stores. There is an interesting museum of local history in the Old Guildhall in Higher Market Street. Looe is Cornwall's second largest fishing port and the fishing industry brings a maritime bustle to the harbour and quayside at East Looe. Looe's viewpoint, Banjo Pier, can be reached from the quay and the very popular East Looe Bay beach adjoins it.

West Looe was always the smaller settlement. It has a lovely outlook across the harbour to East Looe and the older parts of the town around Fore Street and Princes Square have some pleasant features. There is a big car park on the west side of the river at Millpool where there is a Discovery Centre.

The delightful Kilminorth Woods are reached easily from the Millpool car park. Waymarked walks lead through a splendid oak wood and alongside the West Looe River. The woods and river are rich in plant, insect and bird life. These include herons, which nest in the trees on the opposite bank. Further information can be obtained at the Discovery Centre.

LOSTWITHIEL MAP REF SX1059

The attractive little town of Lostwithiel was a busy port throughout the medieval era until the silting of the river stopped vessels reaching its quays. Today the river is spanned by a 13th-century bridge with five pointed arches. Like Liskeard, Lostwithiel was a Coinage town, which prospered greatly from the

revenue earned from the lucrative administration of tin assaying and approval by royal seal. Near by are the substantial ruins of Restormel Castle (English Heritage), the best preserved military building in Cornwall. The castle was built during the Norman period on the site of a wooden fortification.

Modern Lostwithiel has lost much of its old townscape; the arches and buttresses of the Duchy Palace on Quay Street are all that are left of a much grander complex of buildings, which included the Coinage Hall. One special glory is the 13th-century tower and 14th-century spire of the Church of St Bartholomew; the dramatic transition from square shape to octagon has a pleasing effect. There is a town museum in Fore Street. Coulson Park is by the River Fowey and there are pleasant riverside walks.

POLPERRO   MAP REF SX2051

The village of Polperro rambles delightfully down to the sea. The pattern of narrow lanes and alleyways and steep flanking streets is set by the enclosing walls of the wooded valley within which Polperro lies and is more engaging than in any other Cornish village. The inner harbour sits squarely among houses, and the boisterous stream, known as the Rafiel, pours into it beneath a Saxon bridge and beside the delightful House On The Props with its rough wooden supports. Polperro was always a fishing village, and remains so today, though its charm has made it one of the most visited places in Cornwall. Access to Polperro is on foot from a car park at

■ Activity

THE LOOE VALLEY LINE
A trip on the Looe Valley Line from Liskeard to Looe is a stress-free way of going to the seaside and back, recapturing some of the excitement of those days when such a journey as this was a rare treat. The trains descend through the lovely East Looe Valley from Liskeard Station, with station halts on the way giving access along narrow lanes to pleasant villages such as St Keyne.

Crumplehorn above the main village. There are numerous shops, art and craft galleries, restaurants and pubs.

RAME HEAD   MAP REF SX4147

Rame Head is the dramatic western promontory of the Rame Peninsula; it has the well-preserved remains of a typical Iron Age fort. A medieval chapel and a hermitage once stood here and a small building survives, its roof mottled with moss and lichen, its walls rough with age. A warning beacon was once maintained on Rame Head as an aid to navigation, but tradition speaks of its more likely use by smugglers.

From Rame Head, the great crescent of Whitsand Bay curves to the west. The beach is accessible only at low tide and ways down by steep steps and pathways are limited. Above Whitsand Bay, in a crook of the coast road, is Tregantle Fort, the most westerly of the line of defences that march from Fort Bovisand on the Devon shore of Plymouth Sound through a series of surviving bulwarks. They were built in the 1860s in response to fears of French invasion.

A Coastal Walk near Polruan

This lovely woodland and coastal walk starts from the village of Polruan through the ancient parish of Lanteglos. The route wanders through peaceful countryside that was once owned by wealthy medieval families who played a major part in the freebooting activities of Polruan seamen. Original fortunes made through piracy were turned to legitimate trade and to farming and land management. The delightful countryside is the product of long-term land ownership and rural trade. At its heart lies the splendid Lanteglos Church of St Winwaloe, or St Willow. The second part of the walk leads back to the sea, to the steep headland of Pencarrow and to the dramatic amphitheatre of Lantic Bay with its splendid beach. From here, the coastal footpath leads back to Polruan and the busy estuary of the River Fowey.

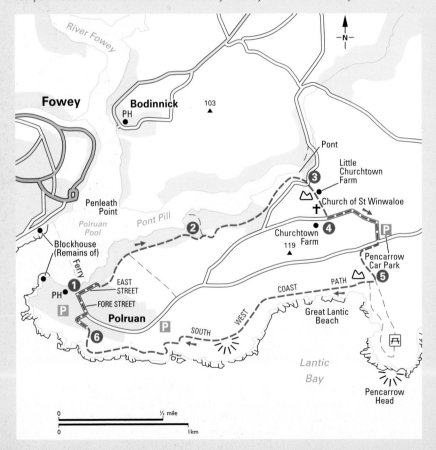

Route Directions

1 Walk up from the Quay at Polruan, then turn left along East Street, by a telephone box and a seat. Go right, up steps, signposted 'To the Hills' and 'Hall Walk'. Go left at the next junction, then keep along the path ahead. Keep right at a junction and pass a National Trust sign, 'North Downs'.

2 Turn right at a T-junction with a track, then in just a few paces, bear off left along a path, signposted 'Pont and Bodinnick'. Reach a wooden gate on to a lane. Don't go through the gate, but instead bear left and go through a footgate. Follow a path, established by the National Trust, and eventually descend steep wooden steps.

3 At a T-junction with a track, turn right and climb uphill. It's worth diverting left at the T-junction to visit Pont. On the route, reach a lane. Go left for a few paces then, on a bend by Little Churchtown Farm, bear off right through a gate signed 'Footpath to Church'. Climb steadily to reach the Church of St Winwaloe.

4 Turn left outside the church and follow a narrow lane. At a T-junction, just beyond Pencarrow car park, cross the road and go through a gate, then turn right along the field-edge on a path established by the National Trust, to go through another gate. Turn left along the field-edge.

5 At the field corner, turn right on to the coast path and descend very steeply. (To continue to Pencarrow Head go left over the stile and follow the path on to the headland. From here the coast path can be rejoined and access made to Great Lantic Beach.) Follow the coast path for about 1.25 miles (2km), keeping to the cliff edge ignoring any junctions.

6 Where the cliff path ends, go through a gate to a road junction. Cross the road then go down School Lane. Turn right at 'Speakers Corner', then turn left down Fore Street to reach the Quay at Polruan.

Route facts

DISTANCE/TIME 4 miles (6.4km) 3h30

MAP OS Explorer 107 St Austell & Liskeard

START Polruan – park on The Quay; grid ref: SX 126511

TRACKS Good throughout, can be very muddy in woodland areas during wet weather

GETTING TO THE START Polruan can be reached via narrow lanes from Polperro and the A390 at Lostwithiel, via Lerryn and Penpoll. Alternatively, take the vehicle ferry from Fowey to Bodinnick, or park in Fowey (on the A3082 to the east of St Austell) and take the passenger ferry across the estuary to Polruan. Pay-and-display parking on The Quay in Polruan.

THE PUB Lugger Inn, Polruan. Tel: 01726 870007; www.staustellbrewery.co.uk

❶ One steep descent on exposed coast path

What to look for

Spend some time exploring Polruan. This fine little port has retained much of its vernacular character in spite of some modern development. Polruan thrived because of seagoing and there is still a rich sense of those sea-dominated days in the narrow alleyways of the village. Also, the handsome Church of St Winwaloe, or St Willow, is where the novelist Daphne du Maurier was married in 1932.

■ TOURIST INFORMATION CENTRES

Fowey
5 South Street.
Tel: 01726 833616;
www.fowey.co.uk

Liskeard
Foresters Hall, Pike Street.
Tel: 01579 349148;
www.liskeard.gov.uk

Looe
The Guildhall, Fore St, East
Looe. Tel: 01503 262072;
www.looe.org

Lostwithiel
Community Centre, Liddicoat
Road. Tel: 01208 872207;
www.lostwithieltic.org.uk

■ PLACES OF INTEREST

Antony House
Torpoint. Tel: 01752 812191

Carnglaze Slate Caverns
St Neot. Tel: 01579 320251;
www.carnglaze.com

Cotehele
St Dominick, near Calstock.
Tel: 01579 351346;
www.nationaltrust.org.uk

Fowey Aquarium
Town Quay.
Tel: 01726 816188;
www.visit-fowey.com

Fowey Museum
Town Hall, Trafalgar Square.
Tel: 01726 833513; www.
museumsincornwall.org.uk

**Daphne du Maurier's
Smugglers at Jamaica Inn**
Tel: 01566 86250;
www.jamaicainn.co.uk

Liskeard Museum
Foresters Hall, Pike Street.
Tel: 01579 346087

Lanhydrock
Bodmin.
Tel: 01208 265950; www.
nationaltrust.org.uk

Looe Valley Line
Liskeard–Looe, with request
stops. Tel: 08457 484950

Lostwithiel Museum
Fore Street. Free.

Lynher Valley Dairy
Upton Cross, near Liskeard.
Tel: 01579 362244

Minions Heritage Centre
Minions.
Tel: 01579 362350

The Monkey Sanctuary
Murrayton, Looe.
Tel: 01503 262532; www.
monkeysanctuary.org

Mount Edgcumbe House
Cremyll.
Tel: 01752 822236; www.
mountedgcumbe.gov.uk

Old Guildhall Museum
Higher Market Street, East
Looe. Tel: 01503 263709

Restormel Castle
Lostwithiel.
Tel: 01208 872687; www.
english-heritage.org.uk

Saltash Heritage Museum
17 Lower Fore Street.
Tel: 01752 848466; www.
saltashheritage.org.uk. Free.

**South-east Cornwall
Discovery Centre**
Millpool, West Looe.
Tel: 01503 262777

Tamar Valley Line
Gunnislake–Plymouth, via
Calstock. Tel: 08457 484950;
www.tamarvalley.org.uk

■ FOR CHILDREN

**Land of Legend and
Model Village**
Polperro. Tel: 01503 272378

**Paul Corin's Magnificent
Music Machines**
St Keyne Station, between
Liskeard and Looe.
Tel: 01579 343108;
www.paulcorinmusic.co.uk

**Porfell Animal Land
and Wildlife Park**
Lanreath, near Lostwithiel.
Tel: 01503 220211;
www.porfellanimalland.co.uk

Tamar Valley Donkey Park
St Ann's Chapel, Gunnislake.
Tel: 01822 834072;
www.donkeypark.co.uk

■ SHOPPING

Fowey
Antiques shops, galleries and
craft shops, Fore Street area.

Liskeard
Open-air market with farm
produce a speciality, Dean
Street Cattle Market, Mon
and Thu.
Trago Mills Shopping Centre
Two Waters Foot. Shopping
complex on the A38, 4 miles
(6.4km) west of Liskeard.

Lostwithiel
Antiques shops in Fore
Street.

■ LOCAL SPECIALITIES

POTTERY

Fowey Pottery
10a Passage Street, Fowey.
Tel: 01726 833099

Millstream Pottery
19 North Street, Fowey.
Tel: 01726 832512

Louis Hudson Pottery Ltd
Unit 8–10, Moorswater
Industrial Estate, Liskeard.
Tel: 01579 342864

The Pottery Shop
Quay Road, Polperro.
Tel: 01503 272307

PERFORMING ARTS

Sterts Open-Air Theatre
Upton Cross, Liskeard.
Tel: 01579 362382;
www.sterts.co.uk

■ SPORTS & ACTIVITIES

ANGLING

Sea
Day and half-day trips from
Fowey, Looe and Polruan.
Shark-fishing from Looe.
Tel: 01503 264355;
www.looechandlery.co.uk

Fly
East and West Looe rivers.
Permits from Looe sub Post
Office. Tel: 01503 262110.
Siblyback Water Park.
Permits available on site.
Ranger Tel: 01579 346522

BEACHES

*Lifeguards, where indicated,
are on summer service. Dogs
are not allowed on several
popular beaches from Easter
Day to 1st October. During
winter, when dogs are allowed,
owners must use poop scoops.*

Kingsand and Cawsand
Small safe beaches.

Looe Hannafore Beach
Shingle and some sand.

East Looe and Plaidy Beach
Popular beach.

Millendreath Beach, near
Looe. Close to Millendreath
Holiday Park.

Seaton Beach
Sand and pebble beach.

Whitsand Bay
Sandy beach but with limited
and steep access. Currents
can make bathing unsafe.

BOAT TRIPS

Calstock
Tamar River cruises.
Plymouth Boat Cruises.
Tel: 01752 408590;
www.soundcruising.com

Fowey
River cruises, motor boat
hire. Information from TIC
(see page 36).

Looe
Sea cruises from harbour.

Morwellham Quay
Canoe Tamar.
Tel: 01822 833408;
www.canoetamar.co.uk

■ COUNTRY PARKS & WOODS

Cardinham Woods
Bodmin. Tel: 01208 72577;
www.forestry.gov.uk/
cardinham

Kilminorth Woods
Discovery Centre, Millpool
car park. Tel: 01503 262777

Kit Hill Country Park
Callington.
Tel: 01579 370030

**Mount Edgcumbe
Country Park**
Cremyll. Tel: 01752 822236;
www.mountedgecumbe.gov.uk

CYCLE HIRE

Liskeard
Liskeard Cycles, Pig Meadow
Lane. Tel: 01579 347696

Looe
Looe Mountain Bike Hire.
Tel: 01503 263871

HORSE-RIDING

Liskeard
TM International School of
Horsemanship, Henwood.
Tel: 01579 362895; www.
tminternational.co.uk

■ EVENTS & CUSTOMS

Fowey
Daphne du Maurier Festival
of Arts and Literature, May.
Fowey Regatta, Aug.

Liskeard
Carnival Week & Agricultural
Show, Jun.

Looe
Carnival Week, Jul/Aug.

Polperro
Arts Festival, Jun.

St Germans
Port Eliot Festival (annual
celebration of words, music,
imagination, laughter,
exploration and fun), Jul.

Tea Rooms

The Plantation

**The Coombes,
Polperro PL13 2RG
Tel: 01503 272223**

A traditional Victorian tea room on the banks of the River Pol. Beams and a fireplace and create a cosy atmosphere. Friendly service delivers home-made cakes, excellent Cornish cream teas, hearty lunchtime meals and a leafy terrace.

Muffins

**32 Fore Street,
Lostwithiel PL22 0BN
Tel: 01208 872278;
www.muffinsdeli.co.uk**

The Cornish cream teas are hard to beat at this light and spacious tea shop. Tuck into home-made scones, served with their Trewithen clotted cream and jam, all best enjoyed in summer in the lovely walled garden. Local produce features well in freshly prepared hot meals.

Edgcumbe Arms

**Cotehele,
St Dominick PL12 6TA
Tel: 01579 351346;
www.nationaltrust.org.uk**

A National Trust tea room housed in a fine granite building beside the River Tamar on Cotehele Quay. Follow a visit to the medieval house and gardens, or a riverside walk, with soup, a ploughman's, or a cream tea.

Crumpets Tea Shop

**1 Fore Street, Polruan,
Fowey PL23 1PQ
Tel: 01726 870806**

Just a five-minute boat trip across the estuary from Fowey, Crumpets is a traditional tea shop decked out in yellow and blue, with sea-related prints on the walls. Just the ticket for light lunches, home-cooked cakes or a delicious cream tea, served with home-made jam.

Pubs

Crown Inn

**Lanlivery, Bodmin PL30 5BT
Tel: 01208 872707;
www.wagtailinns.com**

A fine 12th-century longhouse on the Saints' Way. The pretty garden overlooks the church. In winter, retreat into the low-beamed bars for a pint of Doom Bar beside a log fire. Changing menus include fresh Fowey fish, crab salad and steak and ale pie.

Halfway House Inn

**Fore Street,
Kingsand PL10 1NA
Tel: 01752 822279;
www.halfwayinn.biz**

Wander down the narrow lanes towards the harbour and you will find this cosy inn among the colour-washed houses. Come for locally caught seafood in the dining room, perhaps roast garlic monkfish and smoked fish platter, and fish soup and ploughman's lunches in the simple, stone-walled bar.

Rashleigh Inn

**Polkerris, Fowey PL24 2TL
Tel: 01726 813991; www.
rashleighinnpolkerris.co.uk**

Literally on the beach in a tiny isolated cove and known locally as the 'Inn on the Beach', Rashleigh Inn is worth seeking out for its magnificent setting. Order a pint of Cornish Knocker and head outside to the terrace where, in the evening, you can watch the sun sink into St Austell Bay. The food focuses on fresh local fish.

The Blue Peter

**Quay Road,
Polperro PL13 2QZ
Tel: 01503 272743**

A tiny unspoiled fishing pub built into the cliffside facing Polperro's harbour. The dark and cosy wood-floored bar oozes character, with flickering candles and walls chock full of fishing paraphernalia. Simple, hearty bar food, tip-top Cornish ales and ciders, and sea views.

North Cornwall

North Cornwall has spectacular stretches of coastline where a ten-minute walk can lead to the solitude of quiet coves and wooded valleys. Yet the region has accessible beaches where even on the busiest days there is room to spare. Padstow, Tintagel and Boscastle each have a unique appeal, and then there are the lonely hills and moorland of Bodmin to explore.

4 Walk start point

1 Cycle start point

1 Tour start point

PADSTOW HARBOUR

Unmissable attractions

North Cornwall's coast seems bigger and wilder than anywhere else in Britain. Dark shattered cliffs rise for hundreds of feet from rocky shores at Boscastle and at the magnificent headlands of Trevose and Tintagel. Yet the wildness of the north coast is tempered by the golden sandy beaches of Newquay and Perranporth and by the cheerful seaside towns of Bude, Padstow and St Agnes. Away from the coast, quiet lanes wander through a mellow countryside between villages and hamlets that seem untouched by time. Further inland lies Bodmin Moor waiting to be explored, a lonely wilderness, where fantastical wind-sculpted slabs and pinnacles of silvery granite are scattered across the hills.

1 **Padstow**
Still a busy fishing port of great character, Padstow's thriving fleet of fishing boats provide locally caught lobsters and crabs for restaurants throughout the country.

2 **Tintagel**
The natural splendour of North Cornwall's spectacular coastline as seen through the archway of Tintagel Castle, King Arthur's legendary Camelot.

3 **Widemouth Bay**
The magnificent arc of Widemouth Bay draws families, who enjoy the wide expanse of beach and exposed rock pools at low tide, and surfers, who come to ride the high rolling waves of the Atlantic. The coastal path on the low cliffs backing the bay provides excellent views.

4 **Launceston Castle**
The impressive ruins of Launceston Castle, built soon after the Norman conquest dominates the town and the surrounding countryside. The castle once controlled the river crossing into Cornwall.

5 **Trevose Head**
The Victorian lighthouse standing on the northwest extremity of the granite headland of Trevose Head, west of Padstow, was built to guide ships sailing in the Bristol Channel.

6 **Port Isaac**
The picturesque harbour at Port Isaac provides shelter for local fishing boats, and has rock pools exposed at low tide.

BODMIN MAP REF SX0667

The small town of Bodmin lies on the southwestern fringe of Bodmin Moor. It hardly seems part of the wild country to which it gives its name, although it clings to its own high hill, The Beacon. Bodmin was once the county town of Cornwall, but has long since relinquished that status to Truro.

The town's development began in the 10th century after the monastery, which was founded by St Petroc at Padstow, was destroyed by aggressive Viking raiders. The monks withdrew inland for safety's sake and established their new religious foundation at Bodmin. They brought the holy remains of St Petroc with them and turned the town into the most important medieval religious site in Cornwall. Bodmin's name derives from 'menegh' meaning monks, and 'bos' meaning abode or dwelling. Augustinian monks later adopted the monastery, Franciscans founded a priory here, and the Shrine of St Petroc transformed Bodmin into a sacred place of pilgrimage.

The Reformation and Henry VIII's Dissolution of the Monasteries brought decline, although Bodmin retained its strategic importance for a time because of its position on the main route through Cornwall. Today, though the town has lost much of its historic status, its robust Cornish character and strong community spirit remain intact. Bodmin is the ideal centre from which to explore north and southeast Cornwall.

Bodmin has some outstanding architecture, including a neoclassical court building dating from 1873 situated in Mount Folly. In Fore Street there are attractive stucco facades and the old cattle market has Doric piers and a frieze of rams' and bulls' heads. The Church of St Petroc is the largest church in Cornwall and has some fine features. Bodmin Museum is in Mount Folly Square, on the site of the old Franciscan Priory, and The Duke of Cornwall's Light Infantry Museum is housed in the keep of the Victorian barracks. The Bodmin and Wenford Steam Railway Station is in St Nicholas Street.

■ Activity

STEAMING UP

The Bodmin and Wenford Railway operates steam trains along a delightful rural line from Bodmin to Bodmin Parkway Station, which is on the main Paddington to Penzance line. A branch line also goes west to Boscarne from where the Camel Trail can be joined. The restored Great Western Railway station in Bodmin is the headquarters and main station of the line. It is reached, from the centre of Bodmin, along St Nicholas Street, the B3268, and connections with main line services can be made at Bodmin Parkway. Passengers for the Bodmin and Wenford Railway are not allowed to park at the main line station.

BOSCASTLE MAP REF SX0990

The sea can surge in and out of Boscastle harbour in a menacing way, entering between looming cliffs of slate and shale. The outer walls of the harbour are always damp with the sea and the salt air. Most of the area is owned by the National Trust, as are the adjoining clifflands of Willapark to the south and Penally to the north.

The blow-hole in Penally Point, the headland on the northern side of the harbour entrance, is known as the Devil's Bellows and when the tidal and sea conditions are right, it throws a spectacular spout of spray across the harbour entrance.

Boscastle was a busy commercial port throughout the 19th century – sea transport was usual throughout north Cornwall until the railway arrived in the 1890s. Up to 200 ships called at Boscastle in any one year, carrying coal and limestone from South Wales, wines and spirits, general goods and even timber from Bristol. Cargoes out of Boscastle included china clay and slate, and manganese from a mine in the Valency Valley above the village. Boscastle harbour was always difficult to enter and sailing vessels had to be towed through the entrance by eight-man rowing boats and by horses on tow paths. When big swells threatened to drive vessels against the walls of the channel, hawser ropes were made fast to the vessel from both shores, where teams of men braced the ropes round granite posts to hold the vessel in mid-channel.

Even on land there was no easy exit out of Boscastle and teams of horses hauled carts up and down the steep roads, which today carry traffic. The valley of the River Valency runs inland from Boscastle through deep woods, a peaceful contrast to the threatening sea.

Boscastle village proper is on the high ground and has some fine old buildings. There is a large car park near the harbour and, following the floods in

Activity

BACK LANES BY BIKE

To the north of Bodmin, narrow winding lanes link the villages of Helland, Helland Bridge, Blisland, St Breward, St Tudy and St Mabyn in a good circular tour. This is an area of peaceful mixed countryside and although divided by the B3266, the network of lanes connect across the main road at various points. The area can be reached from the Camel Trail, and offers some delightful cycling and testing navigation. There are steep inclines to negotiate, but there is always the prospect of a pleasant inn and an occasional cream tea halt along the way to recharge the batteries. There are quiet churches to discover, too.

August 2004, the excellent visitor centre was granted a new harbourside location. On the north side of the harbour a National Trust information centre, café and shop is housed in an old blacksmith's forge. It is from here that you can get details of circular walks, a children's quiz and trail, and information on the local history, geology and wildlife of the area. In dull weather, Boscastle can have a certain eeriness, which may explain the presence of a Museum of Witchcraft by the harbour. The museum is full of wicca-related objects to send a chill down your spine.

On Forrabury Common, to the south of Boscastle, the National Trust has preserved the pattern of Iron Age land tenure, whereby long narrow strips of land were cultivated under a system called 'stitchmeal'. These Forrabury Stitches are still cultivated by tenants.

■ Activity

STRATTON STROLL

Stratton was a prosperous market town for several centuries and its attractive, narrow streets reflect its ancient tradition. Therefore, a quiet stroll through Stratton is very rewarding. The town is reached by turning off onto the Holsworthy road from the A39, just east of Bude. There is a car park at Howells Bridge on the eastern edge of Stratton. From the car park, walk up Spicer's Lane to the church and from there into the centre of the town.

BOSSINEY   MAP REF SX0688

Bossiney, a short distance from busy Tintagel, is a quiet relief from too much Arthurian legend. Much of the coast at Bossiney is in the care of the National Trust. The beach below the cliffs at Bossiney Haven is reached by a steep path where donkeys once carried seaweed up from the beach to be used as fertiliser on neighbouring fields.

A short distance to the east lies Rocky Valley, where the river cuts through a final rock barrier into the sea. At the heart of the valley are the ruins of an old woollen mill. Within the ruins are small maze carvings on natural rock, most likely to be Victorian. Rocky Valley's river can be followed inland through the wooded St Nectan's Glen to St Nectan's Kieve, where a 60-foot (18m) waterfall plunges down a dark, mist-shrouded ravine. A fee is payable to view the falls and there is a tea garden above. The site can be reached by public footpath, which starts behind the Rocky Valley Centre at Trethevy on the B3263, a mile (1.6km) northeast of Bossiney.

BUDE   MAP REF SS2105

There are few more exhilarating beaches than Bude's Summerleaze when the sea rolls on to the sand in long, unbroken waves. The Bude Canal shaped much of the immediate hinterland of Bude Harbour and is now a popular attraction for boating, walking and watching wildlife. The canal was built in the early 19th century to carry calcium-rich sand to inland farms, where it was used to enrich the soil. Bude Canal reached nearly to Launceston, but its full potential was never realised and its use declined by the middle of that century. The history of the canal is illustrated in the Bude-Stratton Museum at the Old Forge on the Lower Wharf.

Bude is a busy, friendly town – The Strand and Belle Vue are the main shopping streets. There is a good visitor centre in the car park near the harbour. A series of easily accessible and attractive beaches stretches north from Bude: Crooklets, Northcott Mouth and Sandy Mouth. The last two are almost covered at high tide. There are pleasant walks along the coast path to the north where the cliff-top area is level, cropped grassland. To the south of Bude, via a scenic road, is the vast expanse of Widemouth Bay.

Bude has few traditional buildings. The town evolved in the 19th century from a small fishing port through the grafting on of functional buildings, first for commerce, then for tourism. Just inland is Stratton. This medieval market town with a history that pre-dates Anglo-Saxon times was once the chief settlement of the area.

BUDE CANAL

A Coastal Route from Crackington Haven

This coastal and inland walk has views of the spectacular north Cornish coast.
Crackington Haven has given its name to a geological phenomenon, the Crackington
Formation, a fractured shale that has been shaped into contorted forms. Along the
open cliff south from Crackington the remarkable geology unfolds. Looking back
from Bray's Point, you see the contortions in the high cliff face of Pencarrow Point
on the north side of Crackington. Soon the path leads above Tremoutha Haven and
up to the cliff edge beyond the headland of Cambeak. A short distance further on
you arrive above Strangles Beach, where again you look back to such fantastic
features as Northern Door. The second part of the walk turns inland and descends
into East Wood and the peaceful Trevigue Valley, much of which is a nature reserve.

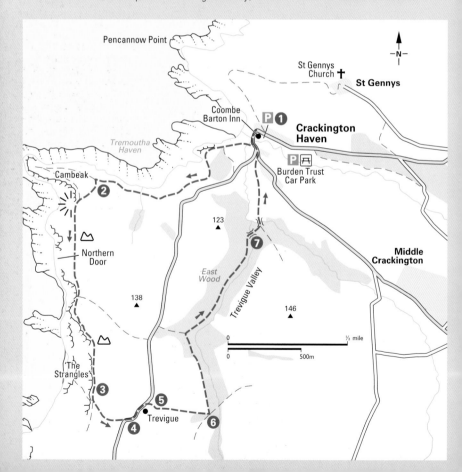

Route Directions

1 From the Crackington Haven car park entrance go left across a bridge, then turn right at a telephone kiosk. Follow a broad track round to the left, between a signpost and an old wooden seat, then go through a kissing gate on to the coast path.

2 Eventually a stile leads to a steep stepped descent to footbridges below Cambeak and a path junction. Keep left and follow a path up a sheltered valley on the inland side of the steep hill, then continue on the cliff path.

3 At the start of a stretch of low inland cliff, pass a coast path post marked 'Trevigue'. Turn left at the next path to reach a road by a National Trust sign for 'Strangles'.

4 Go left, past the farm entrance to Trevigue, then, in a few paces, turn right down a drive by the Trevigue sign. Then bear off to the left across the grass to go through a gate marked with a yellow arrow.

5 Go directly down the field, keeping left of a telegraph pole, to reach a stile. Continue downhill to a stile on the edge of a wood. Continue on down a tree-shaded path to a junction of paths in a shady dell by the river.

6 Turn sharp left here, following the signpost towards Haven, and continue on the obvious path down the wooded river valley.

7 Cross a footbridge, then turn left at a junction with a track. Cross another footbridge and continue to a gate by some houses. Follow a track and then a surfaced lane to the main road, then turn left to the car park

Route facts

DISTANCE/TIME 3.5 miles (5.7km) 1h45

MAP OS Explorer 111 Bude, Boscastle & Tintagel

START Crackington Haven car park (may be busy in high season) or Burden Trust car park, along B3263 to Wainhouse; grid ref: SX 145968

TRACKS Good coastal footpath and woodland tracks, can be very wet and muddy.

GETTING TO THE START Crackington Haven is signposted off the A39 Bude to Wadebridge road at Wainhouse Corner 7 miles (11.3km) south of Bude. It can also be reached from B3263 north of Boscastle.

THE PUB Coombe Barton Inn, Crackington Haven. Tel: 01840 230345

❶ Coast path is very steep in places and close to the cliff edge.

What to look for

The field and woodland section of this walk supports a very different flora to that found on the heathery, windswept cliffland. Some of the most profuse field edge and woodland plants belong to the carrot family, the Umbelliferae. They may seem hard to distinguish, but the commonest is cow parsley, identifiable by its reddish stalk, feathery leaves and clustered white flower heads. Hogweed is a much larger Umbellifer often standing above surrounding plants; it has hairy stalks and broad toothed leaves and can cause an unpleasant rash if it comes in contact with your skin.

■ Activity

CRACKINGTON COAST WALKS

The stretch of coast around Crackington Haven can be reached less strenuously from the sturdy little Church of St Genny's, just north of Crackington Haven. The coast road south of Crackington is well supplied with parking spaces that give access to National Trust cliff land above Strangles Beach. This whole area of cliff has been altered by landslips, and though the coast path is safe and stable, do not stray from it. Just off the coast road is the National Trust farm at Trevigue. Below the farm is a wooded valley through which a fine walk leads down into Crackington Haven.

CRACKINGTON HAVEN

MAP REF SX1496

The mighty and dramatic bulwark of cliff at Crackington is best viewed from the southern approach. It seems to dwarf the cove and beach, its twisted and folded shale mellowed by swathes of grass and sedge. Crackington was a haven of sorts during the 19th century, but it was a port in the most basic sense – small vessels simply ran on to the sand as the tide dropped to offload limestone and coal and to load slates.

The beach at Crackington is rather scant and stony, but the surroundings are pleasant and coastal walks to either side are magnificent. The coast path from Crackington Haven leads north to Castle Point. Take a deep breath for the climb out of the cove. There are the remnants of Iron Age embankments at Castle Point. A mile or so further on is Dizzard Point where an old oak wood clings to the slopes.

DELABOLE MAP REF SX0683

Slate is believed to have been quarried at Delabole as early as medieval times. At 500 feet (152m) this is the deepest quarry in England; it is still being worked and its remarkable proportions can be seen from a public viewing platform. There is a showroom near by. Delabole is a quarrying village with the sturdy character of similar communities in North Wales.

About a mile (1.6km) north of Delabole, along the B3314, is the first commercial wind farm to be established in Britain. The ten great white towers and their whirling vanes are quite sculptural, generating electricity for 3,000 homes. Just south of Delabole is St Teath, a pretty village with an attractive church that has a refreshingly spacious interior.

LAUNCESTON MAP REF SX3384

If Cornwall needs a metaphorical 'gateway', then Launceston, sitting astride the A30, qualifies, castle and all. But take care how you pronounce Launceston: say 'Lanson' – or else. Launceston was once a walled town, known as Dunheved, a powerful Norman stronghold, and the capital of Cornwall.

The legacy of the town's long history is its good architecture and the rather convoluted plan of its streets. To enjoy Launceston, park as soon as you can (there are car parks near the market and at Thomas Road and Tower Street) – Launceston's handsome South Gate forces traffic to pass through in single file while pedestrians pass comfortably three abreast beneath an adjacent arch.

At the centre of the town, the Square has some very fine Georgian buildings, including the White Hart Hotel, which has the added flourish of a Norman arch over its doorway. The entrance to Launceston Castle (cared for by English Heritage) is reached by going down Western Road from the Square. It is impressive still, and though much has been lost, the typical motte-and-bailey structure survives. The stone keep and ruined gatehouse of the motte dominate the highest point of the complex. The clay and rubble walls of the castle seem fragile enough now, but the overall impression is still one of strength and dominance. The Lawrence House Museum in Castle Street, housed in a mid-18th-century building and given to the National Trust to preserve the character of the street, showcases the town's history from the Bonze Age to the Second World War.

In contrast to friable clay, the Church of St Mary Magdalene at Launceston displays dark granite at its ornamental extreme. Every centimetre of this 16th-century building is covered with superbly intricate carving, described by Pevsner as 'barbarous profuseness'. The Launceston Steam Railway is based at the bottom end of St Thomas Road and runs for 2 miles (3.2km) through the valley of the Kensey River. There is an engineering exhibition at the station.

The village of Altarnun lies on the edge of Bodmin Moor about 7 miles (11.2km) west of Launceston. There is a car park just off the A30, from where it is a short walk to the village. The Church of St Nonna, known as the 'Cathedral of

■ Activity

OTTER SANCTUARY
The Tamar Otter Park and Wildlife Centre is situated in North Petherwin, which is reached by turning west off the B3254 at Langdon Cross, about 3 miles (4.8km) north of Launceston. Here, the Otter Trust's aim is to rehabilitate and breed otters for introduction to the wild. Dormice and several species of deer feature amongst other attractions.

■ Insight

JOHN WESLEY AND METHODISM
During the 18th century the uncertainties of the mining and fishing industries resulted in periodic unemployment and hunger in local communities. The established Church was seen as the preserve of the gentry. Amid these negative forces, the natural spirit of the Cornish people survived, but without direction. Violence, drunkenness, neglect and even riot were commonplace. Into this spiritual vacuum came John and Charles Wesley to preach passionately about redemption and non-conformity. Charles Wesley came first, but it was John who made Cornwall his special preserve, visiting about 40 times in 39 years.

the Moor', has a noble tower and a spacious interior with some elegant features. These include a beautifully decorated Norman font and a large number of bench-ends with fine carvings. Cottages and other buildings in Altarnun are very fine. Neville Northey Burnard, the 19th-century sculptor, was born here, and his work can be seen in an early sculpture of the head of John

Wesley, displayed above the door of the old Methodist chapel. He was also responsible for the Lander Memorial at the top of Truro's Lemon Street.

You will find that a fine contrast to Altarnun's 'Cathedral' is the Wesleyan Isbell Cottage at nearby Trewint. Here John Wesley and his fellow preachers stayed during their many visits to Cornwall in the 18th century. Digory Isbell, whose house it was, added a special 'prophet's chamber'. It has now been restored and is still very tranquil.

MORWENSTOW & COOMBE

MAP REF SS2015

The delightful parish of Morwenstow lies at the northern extreme of Cornwall in the narrow corridor of land that the infant Tamar River withholds from its Devon neighbour. Its coast is awesome,

yet unexpected, when approached across the flat green fields that end without much warning at the edge of 300-foot (91.5m) cliffs. This is the land of the famous Culm Measures, great twisted slabs of layered shale that rise from remote boulder beaches that are ribbed with fins of sea-washed rock.

Its natural beauty apart, Morwenstow owes much of its fame to the reputation of the Victorian parson, eccentric and unsuccessful poet, Robert Stephen Hawker, who was vicar at the Church of St Morwenna for many years. The church has good Norman features and is beautifully situated among trees in a shallow combe that leads towards the sea. The interior of the church has great repose and is pleasantly melancholic, especially at dusk, when there is a wonderful feeling of isolation. Visit Morwenstow with time to spare. The land around the church, and the stretch of cliffs to the west, are owned and conserved by the National Trust.

Southwards from Morwenstow is Coombe hamlet, set in a shady wooded valley that continues the theme of peace and tranquillity. The river reaches the sea at Duckpool where the pebble beach has built up to dam a small pool of fresh water. Just north of Coombe, the coast path passes above Lower Sharpnose Point, where spectacular natural piers of rock jut out into the sea like the massive walls of ruined temples.

Inland the smooth satellite dishes of the Cleave Camp Satellite Station strike an incongruous note amidst such raw natural beauty, and dominate the view for miles around.

■ Insight

MORWENSTOW'S VICAR

Morwenstow's Victorian vicar, Robert Stephen Hawker, was a rather eccentric character, devoted to recovering the bodies of drowned sailors – in no short supply along this treacherous coast. But his stay at Morwenstow was fruitful in other ways. Rev. Hawker is credited with reintroducing Harvest Festival celebrations into the church, and wrote the 'Song of the Western Men', now Cornwall's anthem, especially at rugby matches. Hawker built a new vicarage – three of its chimneys were modelled on the towers of favourite churches; another on the tower of an Oxford college. The kitchen chimney was a model of his mother's tomb. While the chimneys smoked, Hawker is said to have smoked opium. He also dressed up as a mermaid on occasions. Say no more!

Along Bude Bay

A pleasant stroll through coastal heathland where the cliff edges provide a refuge for masses of wild flowers. The windswept coastal grasslands of north Cornwall seem unlikely havens for plant life, but, around Bude, the cliff edges especially provide a unique refuge for wild flowers. This walk follows the flat cliff land north of Bude with an inland section on the return. Along the way you'll find numerous wild flowers that turn the cliff-top into a riot of colour in spring and early summer, and butterflies. Look out for the meadow brown, probably Britain's commonest butterfly, the common blue, a small butterfly with an almost lilac tinge, and for the glamorous painted lady with its tawny-orange wings and black and white markings.

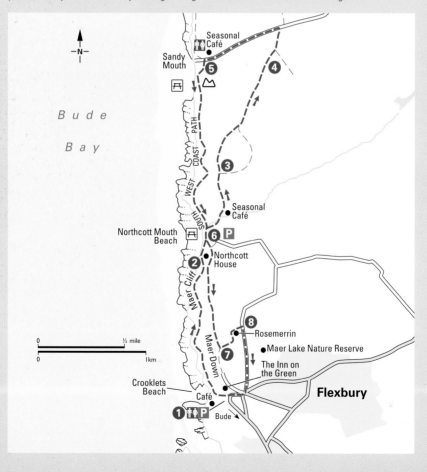

Route Directions

1 From Crooklets Beach car park, go towards the beach, turn right to cross a bridge and head for some steps. Pass behind some beach huts, then turn left along a stony track between walls. Go up some steps and on to the coast path, signposted 'Maer Cliff'. Follow the coast path.

2 Go through a gate and then walk along a track behind a white building, called Northcott House. Bear off to the left, by a signpost, down a path to reach the sea at Northcott Mouth beach. From here, bear right along a track that will take you back inland, past a group of houses on the left, and continue uphill to pass some more houses.

3 Where the track bends round to the right, leave it and keep straight ahead to an open gateway. Keep walking along a banked bridle path ahead.

4 Reach a field gate and follow a track through fields. Keep ahead at a junction with another track, then continue to a T-junction with a public road. Turn left and walk down the road, with care, to Sandy Mouth.

5 Pass the National Trust information kiosk and descend towards the beach, then go left and uphill and follow the coast path back to Northcott Mouth beach, and a lifeguard hut passed earlier on your route.

6 Follow the roadside path just past the lifeguard hut and then retrace your steps towards Northcott House, which you passed earlier. Go along the track behind the building and then keep ahead along a broad track with a field hedge on your left.

7 As buildings come into view ahead, turn left over a stile with a footpath sign in a wall corner. Follow the field-edge ahead into a hedged-in path. Continue walking between trees to a lane by a house at Rosemerrin. Continue until you reach the road.

8 Turn right along the road, with Maer Lake Nature Reserve down to your left. Follow the road to a crossroads and turn right to return to the car park.

Route facts

DISTANCE/TIME 5 miles (8km) 2h30

MAP OS Explorer 111 Bude, Boscastle & Tintagel and 126 Clovelly & Hartland

START Crooklets Beach car park; grid ref: SS 204071

TRACKS Excellent throughout, grassy coast path, field paths and metalled lanes. The National Trust is carrying out regeneration of some eroded sections; please heed notices.

GETTING TO THE START
Follow signs off the A39 for Bude. Go through the town centre and follow signs for Crooklets and Poughill. Turn left at Flexbury on the northern edge of Bude for Crooklets Beach. Large pay-and-display car park by the beach.

THE PUB The Inn on the Green, Flexbury. Tel: 01288 356013

❶ Keep well back from the cliff edges

The Camel Trail – Edmonton to Padstow

Fabulous views, wonderful birdlife and unusual maritime plants make this section of the Camel Trail a delight at any time of year. If you want to keep away from the crowds, turn round on the edge of Padstow, or just dive in quickly for an ice cream.

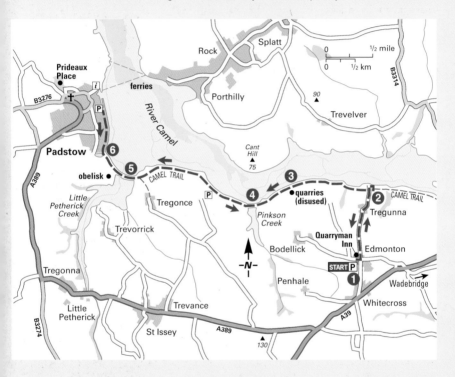

Route Directions

1 The Quarryman Inn is a fascinating place. Behind the pub are two terraces of stone cottages, originally homes for workers at the quarries (Point **3**); when these fell into disuse in the early 20th century the building became a TB isolation hospital. Today it is a very welcoming pub. From

the car park turn right. At the crossroads turn left and enjoy a lovely downhill run, with increasingly good views over the River Camel and farmland beyond. The Camel was known as the Allen River until 1870, thought to derive from the Irish word 'alain', for beautiful: it's clear to see why.

Pass through the hamlet at Tregunna and follow the lane over a bridge to its end. Turn right down a narrow earthy path to reach the trail.

2 Turn right and follow the trail along the edge of the estuary. At low tide it's almost like cycling along the edge of a beach as the river is flanked by broad expanses of sand and the views are superb. The creeks and sandbanks attract wintering wildfowl – widgeon, goldeneye, long tailed duck – as well as many divers and waders, spring and autumn migrants. On route, look out for curlew, oystercatcher, shelduck and little egret. One of the main reasons for constructing the railway was to transport sea sand, which is rich in lime, from the estuary to fertilise farmland away from the coast. Granite, slate, tin, iron and copper from mines on Bodmin Moor were exported.

3 A long cutting ends at the spoil heaps of the old slate quarries, with rounded, wooded Cant Hill opposite. The estuary is widening as it approaches the sea; there's a glimpse of Padstow ahead on the left bank. The mouth of the Camel Estuary is marred by the notorious Doom Bar, a shifting sandbank responsible for more than 300 shipwrecks from 1760 to 1920. If you're cycling the Camel Trail on a sunny day it's hard to imagine such disasters.

4 Continue past Pinkson Creek – you may see herons – and continue on to pass the parking area at Oldtown Cove.

Once through the next cutting you'll get fantastic views towards Rock, on the other side of the estuary, with Brea Hill and Daymer Bay beyond, and out to the open sea. The trail bears away from the estuary through a cutting.

5 Cross the bridge over Little Petherick Creek. The Saints' Way, a 30-mile (48km) walking route, links Fowey on the south coast with Padstow's St Petroc's Church. It runs along the edge of the creek and past the obelisk (commemorating Queen Victoria's jubilee in 1887) on Dennis Hill, seen ahead. The creek is also an important habitat for little egret and a good range of wading birds.

6 Follow the trail past a lake on the left and then past houses on the edge of Padstow, with moored boats on the water on the right. Rock, opposite, is a popular sailing and watersports venue, and there's always masses to watch on the water. The trail ends at the quay and car park; you should dismount at this point to explore the town. Retrace your tracks along the Camel Trail to Edmonton.

Route facts

DISTANCE/TIME 10 miles (16.1km) 2h

MAP OS Explorer 106 Newquay & Padstow

START Quarryman Inn, Edmonton; grid ref: SW 964727

TRACKS Well-surfaced former railway track

GETTING TO THE START Edmonton is west of Wadebridge. Bypass Wadebridge on the A39 signed 'St Columb Major/Padstow'. Approximately 1 mile (1.6km) after crossing the Camel turn right, before Whitecross, on a lane signed 'Edmonton'.

THE PUB Quarryman Inn, Edmonton. Tel: 01208 816444

CYCLE HIRE Camel Trail Cycle Hire, Wadebridge. Tel: 01208 814104; www. cameltrailcyclehire.co.uk

❶ Padstow is always very busy at holiday times – leave your bikes at the secure lock-up on the quay and go into town on foot.

PADSTOW   MAP REF SW9175

Padstow is a likeable, good-natured town in a fine position on the Camel Estuary. Its maritime history is a noble one, though it was often tragic. The shifting sand bar across the mouth of the estuary, the Doom Bar, is extremely dangerous at certain states of the tide and in heavy seas. Records show that more than 300 vessels were wrecked here between 1760 and 1920. At low tide, a vast expanse of sand sweeps away from Padstow, shading to gold towards the sea and to honey-coloured mud towards the inner estuary and Little Petherick Creek. Padstow's busy harbour has been modernised, but in keeping with traditional style. The buildings that cluster around it have great variety, and the maze of streets and narrow passageways behind it are pleasantly cool on sunny mornings. Padstow was a busy trading port from the earliest times, and Welsh and Irish saints of the Dark Ages landed here. St Petroc arrived from Wales in the 6th century and stayed for 30 years, founding a monastery, which thrived until 981 when it was destroyed by marauding Vikings. The present Church of St Petroc is pleasantly sombre within its shaded churchyard. The route of the old railway line, closed in 1967, is now the Camel Trail, a walking and cycle route. North of Padstow is Stepper Point, the fine headland at the entrance to the estuary.

The Saints' Way, Forth an Syns in Cornish, is a 28-mile (45km) route from Padstow to Fowey. It is a delightful route that can be walked in two days and is best started at the Church of St Petroc, Padstow. The first part of the walk to Little Petherick, 2 miles (3.2km) south of Padstow, is worth doing for its own sake. Signposting throughout is generally good; the motif of a stylised Celtic cross is used on wooden posts.

TINTAGEL   MAP REF SX0588

Tintagel should not be missed, even if a visit is fleeting. The focus of this relentlessly 'themed' village is the ruined castle moulded to the blunt summit of 'the Island' of Tintagel Head and approached across a narrow neck of land. The castle is 13th century, but the romance of the site has attracted competing claims for its origins: Iron Age enclosure, Celtic monastery, Roman signal station and, of course, the court of King Arthur. The prominence of the Island suggests that it was used as a defensive site from the earliest times.

Barras Nose to the north and Glebe Cliff to the south are in the care of the National Trust. It is tempting to say that the hinterland is in the care of the King Arthur industry, but Tintagel village offers much more than that. The wonderfully antiquated Old Post Office (National Trust) at the heart of the village is a delightful building. It is actually a small 14th-century manor house, with a central hall rising the full height of the building, and became a post office only in Victorian times. King Arthur's Great Halls in Fore Street is a remarkable token of dedication to a theme. The building was completed in the early 1930s and is devoted to Arthurian memorabilia and includes a collection of stained-glass windows.

Bodmin Moor and the North Coast

This drive takes in the wildest and loveliest parts of Bodmin Moor, including remains of Bronze Age circles, with a visit to the north coast by way of contrast.

Route Directions

Start at Launceston, once a Norman fortified town and now home to fine architecture and interesting little streets.

1 Leave Launceston on the A388 (A30) signed 'Bodmin'. Go under the A30 then, at a roundabout, take the third exit, signed 'South Petherwin B3254'. Pass through South Petherwin and keep on the B3254 to a crossroads with the B3257 at Congdon's Shop (there's a war memorial opposite). Keep ahead for 5 miles (8km), passing through Middlewood and Darleyford, to a crossroads at Upton Cross. Turn right on to an unclassified road, signed 'Minions, Siblyback Lake'. Pass through Minions (parking). Keep ahead at the next junction, signed 'St Cleer', passing a road on the right to Siblyback Water Park.

The watersports centre at Siblyback Lake (toilets) offers windsurfing, kayaking, canoeing and rowing. Tuition is available as well.

2 Continue on the main route, passing King Doniert's Stone on the left (parking). At the next junction, turn right, signed 'Draynes, Golitha Falls'. After 300 yards (274m), a left turn over a bridge leads to a car park (toilets).

From here, it is a short walk to the spectacular Golitha Falls, a National Nature Reserve.

3 Continue to Bolventor. Just before a junction is Daphne du Maurier's Smugglers at Jamaica Inn Centre. At the junction turn left to Jamaica Inn, then left opposite the Inn, signed 'Dozmary Pool'. In 1.5 miles (2.4km) pass Dozmary Pool and around the edge of Colliford Lake (park at Colliford Dam). At a junction turn right, signed 'Bodmin'. Continue to the A30. Turn left, signed 'Bodmin'.

If you can, take a brief detour to Dozmary Pool, said to be final resting place of Excalibur.

4 After 7 miles (11.2km), bear left on to the A389, signed 'Bodmin'. Keep ahead for Bodmin, ignoring left-hand routes, then turn right at a junction, signed 'Bodmin A389'. At a mini-roundabout, go right and along Pool Street and on through

Bodmin following signs for Wadebridge, A389. At a junction, turn right by a clock tower, signed 'Wadebridge' and continue on the A389 for 6 miles (9.6km). At a roundabout take the first exit signed 'Rock, Polzeath'. Turn right at the next roundabout on to the B3314, signed 'Rock, Polzeath'. Cross the Trewornan Bridge, then after 2 miles (3.2km) turn left, signed 'Rock, Trebetherick'. Continue for 2 miles (3.2km), then opposite a garage turn right into Trewint Lane, signed 'Trebetherick, Polzeath'. In 0.75 miles (1km), turn left at the next junction, signed 'Trebetherick, Polzeath'. Pass through Trebetherick and descend steeply into Polzeath, then ascend even more steeply.

If you are a surfer, you might like to detour to Polzeath.

5 In 1.25 miles (2km) pass a turn-off to New Polzeath. Pass a left turn to Portquin, then keep left off the bend, signed 'St Endellion, Port Isaac'. Soon join the B3314 and go left. Continue through St Endellion, then turn left

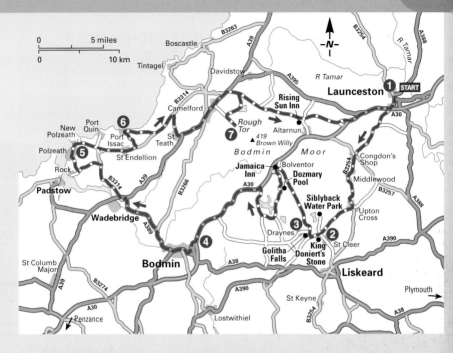

on to the B3267, signed 'Port Isaac'. Go through the upper part of Port Isaac, (park here to visit the village – toilets). Port Isaac is popular and, because the car is sidelined, can claim to be 'unspoiled'. The houses are crowded together with only narrow passageways, called 'drangs', between. The narrowest is Squeeze Belly Alley.

6 Leave Port Isaac and then descend steeply to Portgaverne. Ascend steeply, then continue to the B3314. Turn left, signed 'Delabole', and continue for 1.75 miles (2.8km) to a junction with the

B3267. Turn right, signed 'St Teath'. Keep ahead through St Teath, signed 'Camelford'. Descend steeply to a T-junction with the A39 and turn left, signed 'Bude, Camelford'. Go through Camelford and continue along the A39 for 2 miles (3.2km), then turn right, signed 'Roughtor, Altarnun, Crowdy Reservoir'. After a mile (1.6km) turn right, signed 'Crowdy Reservoir', and follow the road (a one-time airstrip), passing Crowdy Reservoir. At a crossroads, turn left, and soon reach a car park below the impressive granite ridge of Rough Tor.

This is a chance to stretch your legs. Leaving the car park you can take one of several paths towards the top of the Tor. You should come prepared for a muddy walk in wet weather.

7 Return to the crossroads, turn right, pass Crowdy Reservoir again, then, at a junction, turn right signed 'Altarnun'. Continue for about 5 miles (8km) to pass the Rising Sun Inn. Keep left and continue ahead, ignoring all side roads. After 3.5 miles (5.6km) pass Polyphant and reach the A30. Turn left and return to Launceston.

■ TOURIST INFORMATION CENTRES

Bodmin
Shire Hall, Mount Folly.
Tel: 01208 76616;
www.bodminlive.com

Bude
The Crescent Car Park.
Tel: 01288 354240;
www.visitbude.info

Camelford
North Cornwall Museum,
The Clease.
Tel: 01840 212954

Launceston
Market Place.
Tel: 01566 772321;
www.visitlaunceston.co.uk

Padstow
North Quay.
Tel: 01841 533449;
www.padstowlive.com

Wadebridge
Rotunda Building, Eddystone
Road. Tel: 01208 813725

■ PLACES OF INTEREST

Arthurian Centre
Slaughterbridge,
Camelford.
Tel: 01840 212450;
www.arthur-online.com.

Bodmin & Wenford Railway
General Station, Bodmin.
Tel: 01208 73666; www.
bodminandwenfordrailway.
co.uk

Bodmin Jail
Berrycoombe Road,
Bodmin.
Tel: 01208 76292

Bodmin Museum
Mount Folly Square, Bodmin.
Tel: 01208 77067. Free.

Bude-Stratton Museum
Lower Wharf, Bude.
Tel: 01288 353576

Delabole Slate Quarry
Pengelly Road, Delabole.
Tel: 01840 212242;
www.delaboleslate.co.uk

Duke of Cornwall's Light Infantry Museum
The Keep, Bodmin.
Tel: 01208 72810

John Betjeman Centre
Southern Way, Wadebridge.
Tel: 01208 812392; www.
johnbetjeman.org.uk. Free.

King Arthur's Great Halls
Fore Street, Tintagel.
Tel: 01840 770526; www.
kingarthursgreathalls.com

Launceston Castle
Launceston.
Tel: 01566 772365

Launceston Steam Railway
St Thomas Road, Launceston.
Tel: 01566 775665;
www.launcestonsr.co.uk

Lawrence House Museum
9 Castle Street, Launceston.
Tel: 01566 773277. Free.

Long Cross Victorian Gardens
St Endellion, near Port Isaac.
Tel: 01208 880243;
www.longcrosshotel.co.uk

The Museum of Witchcraft
The Witches House,
Boscastle Harbour.
Tel: 01840 250111; www.
museumofwitchcraft.com

National Lobster Hatchery
South Quay, Padstow.
Tel: 01841 533877

North Cornwall Museum and Gallery
The Clease, Camelford.
Tel: 01840 212954

Pencarrow House and Gardens
Washaway, near Bodmin.
Tel: 01208 841369;
www.pencarrow.co.uk

Prideaux Place
Padstow.
Tel: 01841 532411;
www.prideauxplace.co.uk

The Tamar Otter Park
North Petherwin, near
Launceston.
Tel: 01566 785646

Tintagel Castle
Tel: 01840 770328;
www.tintagelcastle.co.uk

■ FOR CHILDREN

Colliford Lake Park
Bolventor, Bodmin Moor.
Tel: 01208 821469;
www.collifordlakepark.co.uk

Cornwall's Crealy Great Adventure Park
Tredinnick, Wadebridge.
Tel: 01841 540276;
www.crealy.co.uk/cornwall

■ SHOPPING

Bodmin
Street market, Mount Folly,
Sat morning.

Padstow
Market, Tue; May–Sep.

◼ LOCAL SPECIALITIES

Crafts
The Lower Wharf Gallery,
by Bude Canal.

Pottery
Boscastle Pottery, The Old
Bakery, Boscastle.
Tel: 01840 250291

◼ SPORTS & ACTIVITIES

ANGLING

Sea
Various trips from Padstow
harbour; enquire locally.

Coarse
Tamar Lakes Water Park,
near Bude. Permit required.
Tel: 01409 211514
Crowdy Reservoir, near
Camelford. Tel: 01237 471291

BEACHES
*Lifeguards, where indicated,
are on summer service. Dogs
are not allowed on several
popular beaches from Easter
Day to 1st October. During
winter, when dogs are allowed,
owners must use poop scoops.*

Bude
Crooklets Beach: good
surfing. Lifeguard.

Constantine Bay
Good sandy area. Limited
parking. Lifeguard.

Crackington Haven
Pebbly beach with sand at
low tide. Lifeguard.

Daymer Bay
Sheltered sandy beach with
dunes. Currents can be
dangerous at certain times.

Harlyn Bay
Sheltered sandy beach with
dunes. Lifeguard.

Padstow
Fine beaches but beware of
dangerous tidal currents.

Polzeath, Hayle Bay
Busy family beach. Lifeguard.

Trebarwith Strand
South of Tintagel. Sand and
rocks. Lifeguard.

Trevone Bay
Pleasant sandy cove.
Lifeguard.

Treyarnon Bay
Good family beach. Lifeguard.

Widemouth
Good for families and surfing.
Lifeguard.

BOAT TRIPS

Bude
Rowing boats and canoes for
hire at Bude Canal.

Padstow
Pleasure trips available from
the harbour.

CYCLE HIRE

Bodmin
Bodmin Bikes, Dennison
Road. Tel: 01208 73192

Bude
North Coast Cycles,
2 Summerleaze Avenue.
Tel: 01288 352974

Padstow
Padstow Cycle Hire Ltd,
South Quay.
Tel: 01841 533533;
www.padstowcyclehire.com

Wadebridge
Bridge Bike Hire, Eddystone
Road. Tel: 01208 813050;
www.bridgebikehire.co.uk
Camel Trail Cycle Hire,
Trevanson Street.
Tel: 01208 814104; www.
cameltrailcyclehire.co.uk

HORSE-RIDING

Boscastle
Tredole Trekking, Trevalga,
Boscastle.
Tel: 01840 250495

Bude
Maer Stables, Crooklets.
Tel: 01288 354141

Launceston
Elm Park Equestrian Centre,
North Beer, Boyton.
Tel: 01566 785353

WATERSPORTS

Bude
Outdoor Adventure,
Widemouth Bay.
Tel: 01288 362900; www.
outdooradventure.co.uk

Polzeath
Surfs Up, Polzeath.
Tel: 01208 862003; www.
surfsupsurfschool.com

◼ EVENTS & CUSTOMS

Bodmin
Riding and Heritage Day, Jul.

Bude
Jazz Festival, end of Aug.

Padstow
May Day Festival.

Wadebridge
Royal Cornwall Show, Jun.

NORTH CORNWALL

Tea Rooms

Rectory Farm Tea Rooms

Morwenstow, Bude EX23 9SR
Tel: 01288 331251;
www.rectory-tearooms.co.uk
Dating back to 1296, this working farmhouse offers good honest cooking. Enjoy the peaceful garden on summer days or take refuge in the cosy rooms with big open fireplaces on cold days. Freshly prepared food includes ploughman's platters, soups and pasties, and light, home-baked scones served warm with clotted cream.

The Tea Shop

6 Polmorla Road,
Wadebridge PL27 7ND
Tel: 01208 813331
Fresh local produce takes pride of place on the menu at this bright and cosy tea shop, and everything is prepared on the premises. Expect to choose from a range of 40 teas and around 30 cakes, including boiled fruit cake and apple and almond cake. Light lunches are available.

Rick Stein's Café

10 Middle Street,
Padstow PL28 8AP
Tel: 01841 532700;
www.rickstein.com
The most relaxed of Rick Stein's restaurants is a casual café-with-rooms decked out with a nautical theme. It's open all day, so call in for breakfast or an excellent cappuccino and peruse the papers, or arrive early for deliciously simple lunches and dinners – salt and pepper prawn, whole grilled mackerel with tomato and onion salad, or chickpea, parsley and salt cod stew.

Pubs

Mill House Inn

Trebarwith,
Tintagel PL34 0HD
Tel: 01840 770200;
www.themillhouseinn.co.uk
A converted 18th-century mill house halfway up the wooded valley from the beach at Trebarwith. The bar is big, with flagged floors, a wood-burning stove, and Sharp's ales on tap. In the new contemporary restaurant sample salt and pepper squid and local lamb with sautéed kale.

Bush Inn

Morwenstow, Bude EX23 9SR
Tel: 01288 331242;
www.bushinn-morwenstow.
co.uk
The historic Bush Inn is set in an isolated cliff-top hamlet. Flagstones, beams, inglenooks and old settles preserve the character of the bar. There's a contemporary feel to the dining room which offers dishes such as Thai scallop salad and whole roast John Dory, while traditional ploughman's and cream teas are served in the bar.

Old Inn

Church Town, St Breward,
Bodmin Moor
PL30 4PP
Tel: 01208 850711;
www.theoldinnand
restaurant.co.uk
This low, whitewashed moorland inn has a bar that dates back to the 11th century. The bar sports thick beams, oak settles, slate floors and roaring log fires. The food is wholesome, unpretentious and not for the faint-hearted – portions are very generous.

Rising Sun

Altarnun, Launceston
PL15 7SN
Tel: 01566 86636;
www.therisingsun.co.uk
A rustic, 16th-century former farmhouse hidden down lanes on the edge of Bodmin Moor. Enjoy tip-top beers, lunchtime seafood chowder or crab sandwiches and imaginative evening food, perhaps duck leg confit with sherry sauce, or sirloin steak with red wine sauce.

Mid-Cornwall

The contrast between the north and south coasts of mid-Cornwall is quite dramatic. The north coast – famous for surfing beaches, such as Newquay – is also home to delightful family beaches backed by sand dunes and flanked by magnificent headlands. The south is more placid, its beaches quieter and pleasantly remote, while around Mevagissey and the exquisite Roseland Peninsula, there is a lush quality to the landscape. In the east is St Austell and Cornwall's famous white 'Alps' of the clay country, home of the Eden Project, and, at its heart, the busy cathedral city of Truro.

6 Walk start point

2 Cycle start point

MEVAGISSEY

DODMAN POINT

GREAT WESTERN BEACH

Unmissable attractions

Mid-Cornwall is packed full of delights. In the southwest is St Agnes, a friendly unassuming coastal village surrounded by some intriguing tin-mining remains. Inland lie the old mining towns of Camborne and Redruth, hardly picturesque, but rich in industrial archaeology and home of Cornwall's School of Mines, where there is an excellent geology museum. A few miles north of St Agnes, at Perranporth, is one of Cornwall's vast beaches, where acres of wave-rippled sand are exposed at low tide. Neighbouring Newquay is Britain's premier surfing venue where the magic mix of Atlantic swell and golden sand draws surfers from all over the world. At the heart of this area is the busy city of Truro and its magnificent cathedral.

5

1 The Eden Project
Throughout the Eden Project you will find exciting multimedia and sculptural exhibits depicting the exotic world of plants, their products and habitats.

2 Truro Cathedral
Standing in the heart of the city, the cathedral was built of local granite and Bath stone in the 19th century. Inside, soaring arches and slender pillars, bathed in a golden light, lead the eye up to the vaulted roof.

6

3 Pendarves Woods
This nature reserve, on the outskirts of Camborne, is a mixed broad-leaf woodland with streams and an area of marsh surrounding the lake.

4 Carwinion Garden
This peaceful 12-acre (5ha) garden in Mawnan Smith was created in the 1800s and shelters superb collections of bamboo, camellias, hydrangeas and ferns.

5 Watergate Bay
Surfers come to Watergate Bay, just north of Newquay, to enjoy some of the best waves that Cornwall has to offer.

6 The Lost Gardens of Heligan
Tree ferns, palms and bamboo are among a few of the exotic trees and shrubs that flourish in The Jungle section of the lush green gardens of Heligan.

7

7 Mevagissey
The charm of Mevagissey's narrow streets, old houses and harbour dotted with fishing boats attracts many visitors.

BEDRUTHAN STEPS

MAP REF SW8468

Access to the beach at Bedruthan has been difficult over the years because of the crumbling nature of the cliffs, but the National Trust has built a secure stairway from the clifftop at Carnewas. The famous 'Steps' are the weathered rock stacks that stand in bold isolation amidst the sand. Bedruthan Steps are the result of sea erosion on the caves and arches in the friable slate cliffs. They have colourful local names, such as Queen Bess, Samaritan Island and Diggory's Island. According to local legend, a mythical giant, Bedruthan, was reputed to use the stacks as stepping stones; but to nowhere in particular it seems. There is a National Trust shop and café on the clifftop in what was the office building of the old Carnewas iron mine. This is a delightful spot to indulge, as cream teas and other Cornish treats are the order of the day.

■ Insight

THE CORNISH MINER ABROAD

There is a saying that says at the bottom of a deep mine anywhere in the world, you will find a Cornish miner digging even deeper. There is some truth in this. It was the thousands of miners forced into emigration by mining slumps at home that made the Cornish so famous abroad. A particularly severe slump in copper mining during the 1860s caused many miners to emigrate to the Americas, South Africa and Australia. 'Cousin Jacks', as they were known, either sent money home or brought their families to join them, and Cornish names and traditions still survive in far-flung places.

CAMBORNE   MAP REF SW6440

Camborne is not picturesque and would not thank you for saying otherwise. The town has borne the brunt of Cornish industrialisation and of the strip development that the linear shape of the county dictated, but the town thrives still, in spite of the current cessation of work at the nearby South Crofty tin mine. There are gems of industrial archaeology at Pool, midway between Camborne and Redruth, where the National Trust has restored two great steam engines. They were used for pumping water from a depth of 1,640 feet (500m) and for winding men and ore up and down the mine shafts. Near by is the Industrial Discovery Centre, which provides an overview of Cornwall's industrial heritage and incorporates a fascinating audio-visual presentation.

Camborne was associated with the greatest of Cornish inventors, Richard Trevithick (1771–1833), whose statue stands outside Camborne Public Library in Trevenson Street. Trevithick was born at nearby Illogan. He married a daughter of the Hayle foundry family, the Harveys, and devoted his life to industrial invention and development. Trevithick designed steam engines and invented a steam threshing machine, an early road vehicle, and the first railway engine. Camborne celebrates its famous son with a special Trevithick Day in April. A small museum in the library has displays on mining and archaeology and on Trevithick's work. The nearby Tehidy Country Park has leafy walks, streams and ornamental lakes, and is close to the invigorating north coast.

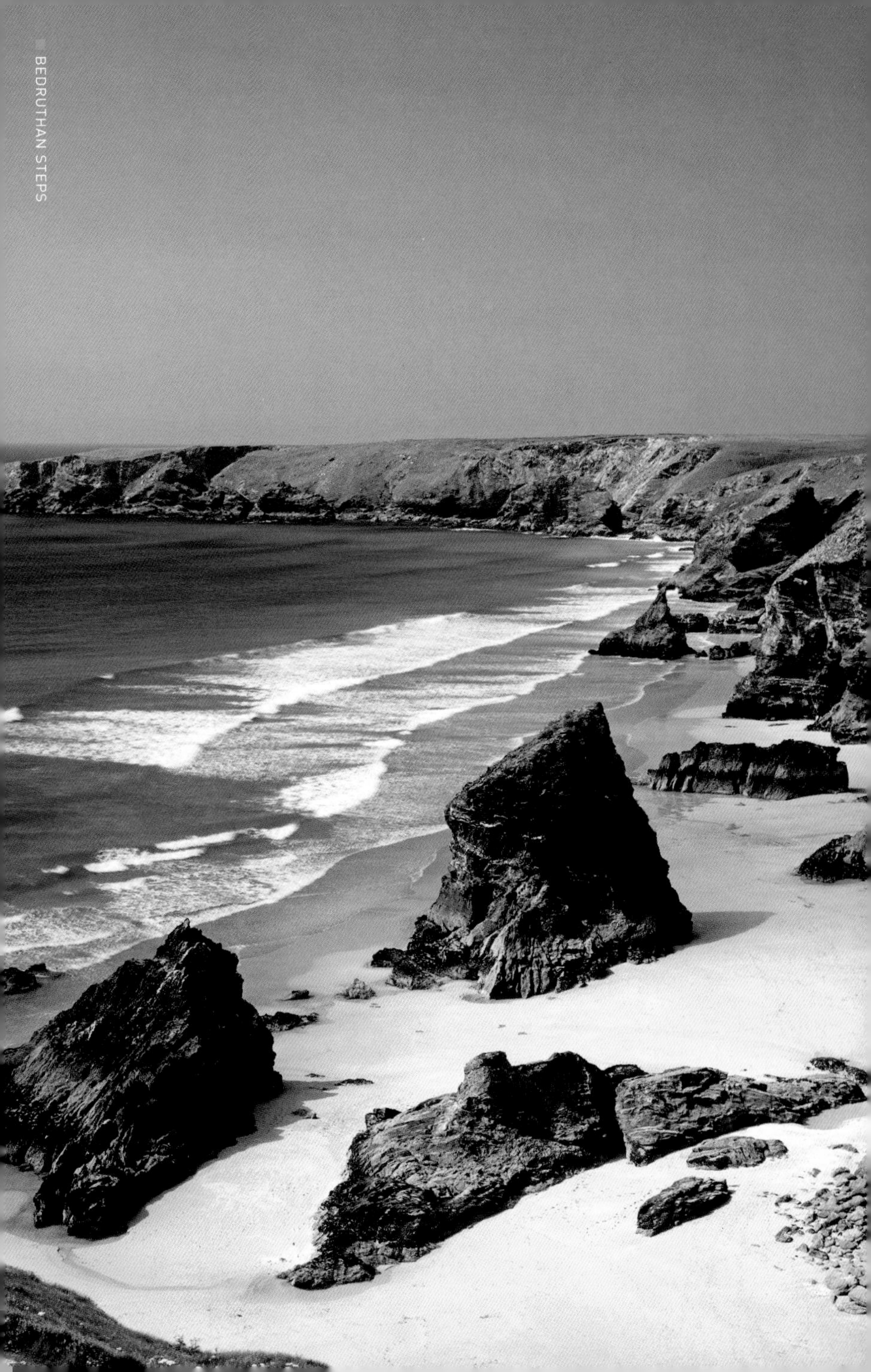
BEDRUTHAN STEPS

St Agnes Head to St Agnes Beacon

This bracing walk along the cliffs at St Agnes is followed by a steady inland climb to the top of St Agnes Beacon and an optional coast-path walk to the pub. Following the flat cliff-top tracks, past the little promontory of Tubby's Head, once an Iron Age settlement, the walk passes through what was once an industrial mining landscape. Beyond Towanroath the path descends into Chapel Porth and a typical Cornish beach. As you walk up the valley, you pick your way through a landscape now overgrown by nature, but that was once subdued by industry. From the valley floor the route leads up a delightful valley, protected from the harsh weather, and soon you climb onto the summit of St Agnes Beacon, a superb viewpoint. From here you drop down to the coast path once more.

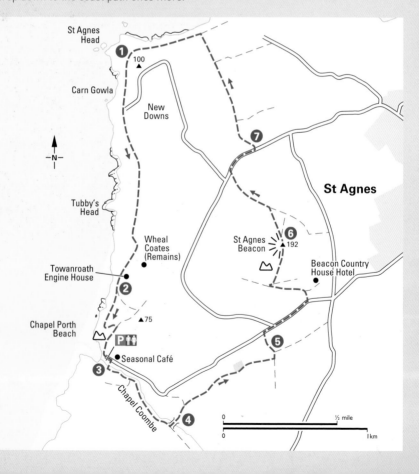

Route Directions

1 Join the coastal footpath from your clifftop parking place at St Agnes Head. Follow the stony track across Tubby's Head. Branch off right on to a narrower path (acorn signpost) about 100yds (91m) before old mine buildings (the remains of Wheal Coates mine). Cross a stone stile and continue to Towanroath mine engine house.

2 About 80yds (71m) beyond Towanroath, branch off right at a junction and continue to Chapel Porth Beach.

3 Cross the stream at the back corner of the car park and follow a path up Chapel Combe. Keep straight ahead when the main path bends sharp right. Pass below a mine building and where the path forks among trees, go left through a wooden kissing gate.

4 Cross a bridge then turn right along a track and where it bends left go right along another track. Pass some houses and where the track narrows to a path, keep ahead at a fork. Go through a gate and pass a bench. Go along the edge of a field and eventually turn left through a kissing gate on to a wide track.

5 At a junction, turn left and then right at Willow Cottage and go up to a public road. Turn right and keep ahead at the next junction. In 200yds (183m), next to the entrance of the Beacon Country House Hotel, go up a stony track on the left. After 50yds (46m), at a junction, turn left. The track becomes a path just past a cottage. At a staggered junction keep straight ahead uphill between telegraph poles to the summit of St Agnes Beacon.

6 From the summit of the Beacon follow the left-hand track of two tracks, heading north-west down to a road. Turn right along the road to reach a seat.

7 Go down the track opposite the seat. Where the track bends right, keep straight on down a path directly to the edge of the cliffs, then turn left at a junction with the coast path and return to the car park. To walk to the Driftwood Spars Hotel at Trevaunance Cove, turn right along the coast path for a mile (1.6km). Return along the coast path back to your car.

Route facts

DISTANCE/TIME 5 miles (8km) 3h

MAP OS Explorer 104 Redruth & St Agnes

START St Agnes Head. Clifftop parking; grid ref: SW 699512

TRACKS Good coastal footpaths and inland tracks

GETTING TO THE START St Agnes is on the B3277 and signposted off the A30, 5 miles (8km) north of Redruth at the junction with the A390. In the village centre, turn left opposite the church, then take the third road right in 1 mile (1.6km) to reach the cliff area parking at St Agnes Head.

THE PUB Driftwood Spars Hotel, Trevaunance Cove (see Point 7). Tel: 01872 552428; www.driftwoodspars.com

❶ Narrow cliff-edge path, old mine workings and one steady climb to the top of St Agnes Beacon.

Mylor Churchtown to Flushing

This walk takes you from Mylor Churchtown along the shores of the blunt headland between Mylor Creek and the Penryn River and on to Flushing, in full view of Falmouth docks. From Flushing you turn inland and walk along a delightful old track that runs down a wooded valley to Mylor Creek and back to St Mylor Church.

Route Directions

1 From the car park entrance, turn right to reach the start of a surfaced lane, signposted to Flushing. Follow the lane, then, by the gateway of a house, bear left along a path. Pass in front of Restronguet Sailing Club and keep to the right of a detached building.

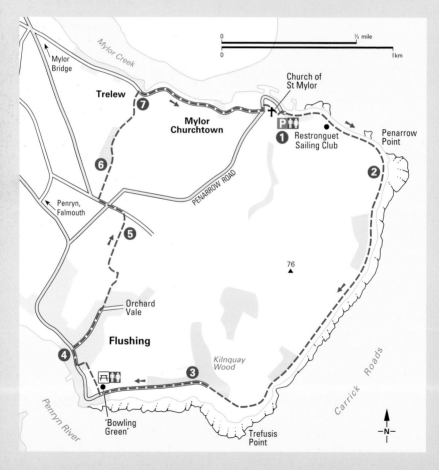

2 Follow the path round Penarrow Point and continue round Trefusis Point. Reach a gate and granite grid stile by a wooden shack at Kilnquay Wood. Continue until you reach a lane.

3 Follow the surfaced lane round left, then go right through a gap beside a gate and continue along a public road. Where the road drops down towards the water's edge, bear right up a surfaced slope to the grassy area of the 'Bowling Green'. (Strictly no dog fouling, please.) Continue past a little pavilion and toilets and go down a surfaced path, then turn left at a junction just after two seats.

4 Turn right at a street junction and go past the Seven Stars Inn. At a junction by the Royal Standard Inn, keep right and go up Kersey Road. At the top of the road, by Orchard Vale, go left up steps, signposted 'Mylor Church'. Cross a stile and keep to the field-edge to reach an isolated house and a stile made of granite bollards.

5 In 25yds (23m) go right through a gate then turn left over a cattle grid and follow the drive to a public road, Penarrow Road. Cross with care, and go down the road

opposite for 30yds (27m), then go right down steps and on down the field-edge.

6 Enter woodland and keep right at a junction to follow a rocky path that is often a mini stream after heavy rainfall. Go through a gate, keep ahead at a junction then cross a small stream. Go through a tiny gate and then turn right down a farm track to reach a surfaced lane at Trelew.

7 Turn right along the lane, passing an old water pump. When you get to a slipway, keep ahead along the unsurfaced track. Continue along between granite posts and on to join the public road into Mylor Churchtown. Cross the road with care (this is a blind corner) and go through the churchyard of St Mylor Church (please note, the path through the churchyard is not a public right of way). Turn right when you reach the waterfront to find the car park in Mylor Churchtown.

Route facts

DISTANCE/TIME 4 miles (6.4km) 3h

MAP OS Explorer 105 Falmouth & Mevagissey

START Mylor Churchtown pay-and-display car park; grid ref: SW 820352

TRACKS Good paths throughout. Wooded section to Trelew Farm is often very wet, 7 stiles

GETTING TO THE START Mylor Churchtown lies east of Penryn and is best reached from the A39 north of Falmouth. In Penryn follow signs along narrow lanes for Flushing and Mylor Churchtown for 3 miles (4.8km). Pass the Church of St Mylor to the waterfront and marina and turn right into the car park.

THE PUB The Seven Stars Inn, Flushing. Tel: 01326 374373; www.sevenstarsflushing.co.uk

CHARLESTOWN MAP REF SX0351

Charlestown is St Austell's gateway to the sea. The creation of the port in the late 18th century was the brainchild of local entrepreneur Charles Rashleigh and became known as 'Charles's town'. The harbour was originally West Polmear, a modest fishing cove where ships ran on to the beach to load copper ore and china clay from the developing industries of the St Austell area. Rashleigh also commissioned Eddystone Lighthouse engineer John Smeaton to build a deep harbour with lock gates.

The road to Charlestown is a fine, broad avenue in keeping with the breadth of Rashleigh's ambitions for the town. Square-rigged ships are now berthed in the harbour and can be visited during the summer. There is a Shipwreck and Heritage Centre and nautical pubs.

Charlestown is a favourite with film makers, and its harbour and sailing ships were used in the 1970s television series *The Onedin Line* and the 1976 film *The Eagle Has Landed*.

CRANTOCK MAP REF SW7960

Crantock stands beside the long, narrow estuary of the River Gannel. At the heart of the village is the serene little Round Garden, now in the care of the National Trust. Crantock also has two holy wells, one in the centre, the other on the road to the beach. The Church of St Carantocus has 13th- and 14th-century features. There are shops and pubs in the village, and a tea garden that is open during the summer. Crantock beach is just west of the village; above the beach is Rushy Green, an area of sand dunes.

To the west of Crantock is West Pentire, where there is a car park. From here you can take the zigzag track south to Porth Joke, also known as Polly Joke, a charming sand-filled cove.

Holywell Bay, further south again, is reached from Crantock by following an unclassified road south to Cubert, from where a right turn leads to the car park above Holywell's sandy beach.

THE EDEN PROJECT
MAP REF SX0555

Cornwall's spectacular 'global garden', the Eden Project, has transformed a one-time clay-quarrying pit at Bodelva near St Austell into one of Europe's most popular tourist attractions. Eden is housed in futuristic glass biomes – enormous domed conservatories within which the main climate systems of the world have been vividly recreated.

Inside the huge Rainforest Biome pathways wind through the plants and products of West Africa, South East Asia, Amazonia, Malaysia and Oceania. There are even teak, mahogany and rubber trees, interspersed with bamboo, a banana plantation, and a host of intriguing tropical plants, all fed by the moisture from a cascading waterfall.

The smaller Mediterranean Biome replicates the habitats of Southern Africa, the Mediterranean and California, with hundreds of vividly coloured flowers intermingled with olive groves and vines. From the main biomes you move into Eden's stunning gardens, covering 30-acres (12ha), where the plants of the West Country flourish alongside those of the Himalayas, Chile and Australasia.

GORRAN HAVEN & THE DODMAN MAP REF SX0141

Gorran Haven lies just south of Mevagissey at the seaward end of a shallow valley. Steep lanes and passageways climb from the harbour and an intriguing little chapel built on solid rock dates from the 15th century. South of Gorran Haven, the mighty Dodman Point thrusts its bull's head into the seaway. The Dodman, as it is commonly known, is 373-feet (114m) high. The Iron Age earthworks that enclose the seaward area of the Dodman are over 2,000-feet (609m) long and 20-feet (6m) high.

MEVAGISSEY MAP REF SX0144

Mevagissey tucks into the land and guards itself within the folded arms of its inner and outer harbours. It is one of Cornwall's most popular resorts, a fishing village whose simple charm attracts tourists in their thousands. It became a leading pilchard fishing port in Tudor times and continued as such into the 21st century. For many years it supplied the navy with pilchards, which became known as Mevagissey Ducks. Today there is still a fishing fleet here but one that is more diverse. Like most Cornish fishing villages Mevagissey has great character, especially in the old part of the village that lies between the Fountain Inn and the Battery on the eastern side of the harbour. Many of the houses are pleasingly colour-washed and despite the fact that the harbour area has seen some rather brutal modern development, the village has retained its Cornish charm.

The inner harbour is a place to linger on warm summer days – seats line the quays but competition is fierce. The narrow alleys and streets of the village draw you on to the next corner, past inviting galleries and gift shops and in and out of light and shade. The aquarium at the old lifeboat house on the South Quay gives an insight into life in deeper waters (the profits go to the upkeep and improvement of Mevagissey harbour). There is a fine little museum of local history on the East Quay and, engagingly for this sea-going town, there is a model railway museum in Meadow Street.

Heligan was once a lost garden, but now has been well and truly found. It lies northwest of Mevagissey and can be reached from the B3273 St Austell road. Restored Victorian features include lakes and ponds, an Italian Garden, an extensive valley garden with a splendid collection of tree ferns, and huge productive gardens and fruit houses.

■ Visit

GODREVY HEAD

The National Trust property of Godrevy Head stands at the eastern end of St Ives Bay and is the first of a sequence of high rugged cliffs of dark slate that run uninterruptedly to the northeast. Offshore from the headland stands Godrevy Island and its crowning lighthouse. There is ample parking at Godrevy Head on grassy downs that are reached along a winding road. Paths lead across and around the headland; the offshore waters attract inquisitive grey seals. To the south lies Gwithian beach, and inland is the village of Gwithian where there is a handsome church and an attractive pub.

MYLOR MAP REF SW8135

Between Truro and Falmouth is the parish of Mylor, dense with trees and bordered by tidal creeks. A network of country lanes north of Falmouth links Mylor Bridge, Mylor Churchtown, Restronguet Passage and Mylor Creek. There was once a royal dockyard at Mylor Churchtown where, during the 19th century, the Falmouth packet ships that delivered mail worldwide were repaired and victualled. The Church of St Mylor is in a superb position and has some unique features – a turret rises from its west gable and it has Norman doorways and a fine interior. The gravestones of Mylor are instructive and entertaining. The headstones of Joseph Crapp, near the east window, and of Thomas James, smuggler, near a fork in the churchyard path, bring a smile to your face. Due south from Mylor Bridge, the attractive village of Flushing faces Falmouth just across the river, and a passenger ferry links the two.

NARE HEAD MAP REF SW9136

Nare Head is the focus of a beautiful stretch of coast that borders the parishes of Gerrans, Veryan and St Michael Caerhays, between the Roseland Peninsula and Dodman Point. The easiest approach to the area is along the A3078, then on an unclassified road that leads to the village of Veryan, noted for its unique and elegant church and for its remarkable thatched round houses. The Church of St Symphorian is impressive, with a dark tower of mottled stone. There are a number of beaches along the shores of Gerrans Bay and Veryan Bay. The best beaches are at Pendower and Carne where there is good parking and access to Nare Head. To the east is the quiet little village of Portloe, which has a small car park at its eastern end. Further east again is a beach at Porthluney below Caerhays Castle, a picturesque, 19th-century replacement for an older building, which has a fine informal woodland garden.

NEWQUAY MAP REF SW8161

Newquay is geared unashamedly to its splendid beaches, of course, and in places there seem to be more hotels and guest houses than breathing space. But there is still a strong sense of the 'old' Newquay. Sea-angling trips are

■ Visit

THE LOST GARDENS OF HELIGAN

The story of the 'lost' gardens of Heligan is compelling. From 1780 onwards, the Tremayne family developed 57 acres (23ha) of their property at Heligan as a series of splendid gardens. Nature began to get a hold on the gardens during the First World War, when the house became a military convalescent home and most of the 22 gardeners enlisted. The house was used again by the American military during the Second World War and was later converted into flats, and though the Tremaynes still owned the gardens, they remained untouched. In 1990 the estate was inherited by John Willis who, with others, including Tim Smit, the moving force behind The Eden Project, made tentative inroads into the impenetrable jungle and discovered the intact framework of a magnificent garden. By the end of 1995 the restoration was complete.

available; a good way of appreciating the marine environment and the sea-going traditions of this Cornish town.

The town is lively. The beaches and broad, busy streets with shops, pubs and clubs make Newquay the epitome of bright and breezy holiday-making. Yet there are quiet corners in flower-filled parks and gardens. Attractions include a zoo and fun pools, and a swimming pool at the Water World in Trenance Leisure Park off Edgcumbe Avenue.

The Elizabethan manor house of Trerice (National Trust) lies just 3 miles (4.8km) south-east of Newquay. It is an exquisite building. The Elizabethan gardens have long since disappeared but the Trust has laid out the south side of the old garden with fruit trees in a classic 17th-century pattern. There is a restaurant in the Barn and a hayloft has a collection of antique lawnmowers.

PERRANPORTH MAP REF SW7554

The Porth of 'Perran' is the small river channel that slices through the sands into Perran Bay. This is proper golden sand country. A great swathe of it runs north from Perranporth and, at low tide especially, offers the pleasure of beach walking into the distance. But don't walk too far – at the northern end of the great beach is a military training area. It is because of the drifting sands here that Perranporth has had three St Piran's churches. The first, dating from the 6th or 7th century, was abandoned as early as the 11th century and, though rediscovered in the 19th century, has been buried again in the sand for its own preservation. The second church was abandoned in the 15th century and the latest was built in a village nearby.

Perranporth is a very pleasant resort, which has benefited from being at the heart of 'Poldark Country', a welcome marketing image drawn from the Poldark novels, which were later adapted into a popular television series, and illustrate what life was like in Cornwall in the late 19th century. The early books in the saga were written by Winston Graham during the time he lived in Perranporth and many local features inspire the books. He developed his image of the Cornish coastline featured in Poldark from a composite of the coast from Perranporth to Crantock, near Newquay. The area of Perranporth itself was the model for Nampara, the fictional setting of the stories.

PROBUS MAP REF SW8947

The village of Probus boasts the tallest church tower in Cornwall. It is more than 123-feet (37.5m) high and is lavishly decorated. The village also boasts one of Cornwall's most interesting gardens. This is Probus Gardens, a demonstration garden of great variety where much good work is carried out and where keen gardeners can pick up a few tips while they enjoy the varied displays of flowers, shrubs, vegetables and fruit. Probus can be reached along the A390 from Truro or St Austell. The garden lies on the St Austell side of the village.

A short distance along the A390 from Probus Gardens is Trewithen Garden surrounding the handsome 18th-century Trewithen House. The house and garden are open to the public.

Through the Pentewan Valley

A ride along the banks of the St Austell River, with an optional extension to the Lost Gardens of Heligan.

Route Directions

1 From the village car park return towards the B3273 and pass through the parking area for Pentewan Valley Cycle Hire, and round a staggered barrier onto the trail, which initially runs levelly through marshy woodland. The trail emerges from shady woods onto the banks of the St Austell River, with a caravan site opposite.

2 Turn right and follow the trail along the river bank. This is a popular stretch with pedestrians. Along part of the trail, walkers have the option of taking a narrow parallel route on a bank.

3 Note the turn-off left across the river to the Lost Gardens of Heligan. Pass round the edge of a small parking area into King's Wood (Woodland Trust), and follow the trail as signed left back onto the riverbank. Dip into woodland again, then bear right, away from the river onto a lane, with a small parking area a little uphill to the right.

4 Turn left; pass a small parking area to meet a tarmac lane on a bend. Bear right as signed. Turn left opposite 'Brooklea' and continue on a narrow wooded path, with a caravan site left. The track bears left at Molingey – with London Apprentice on the other side of the river – then right to run along the right bank of the river again. Continue to follow this tarmac way as it bears right through fields, then left along to reach the edge of the water treatment works. Turn left for 50yds (46m) to meet the B3273. Turn right to walk along the pavement.

5 Cross the lane to Tregorrick, and take the second lane on the right (Sawles Road – unsigned). Follow this quiet country lane to its end. For St Austell (and a possible extension to the Eden Project) turn left uphill to cross the A390. To reach Pentewan either turn around here, or for a more pleasant alternative, turn right and cycle steeply uphill through some pleasant countryside. Drop to a T-junction and turn right, steeply downhill, through Tregorrick. On meeting the B3273 turn left to return to Pentewan on the outward route.

6 Heligan extension: just after passing Point 2, turn right to cross over the river on the footbridge (dismount). At the B3273, turn left. Pass the touring park on the left, then turn right to cross the road as signed. Turn left with the pavement, then continue on a track. This bears right, away from the road into Tremayne Estate woodland. Climb steadily uphill for 0.75 mile (1.2km), levelling off as the track passes beneath a

Route facts

DISTANCE/TIME 7 miles (11.3km) 1h30; including optional extension 10 miles (16.1km) 2h30

MAP OS Explorer 105 Falmouth & Mevagissey

START Pentewan Valley Cycle Hire; grid ref: SX 017473

TRACKS Mainly well-surfaced track, some woodland paths and a little road work

GETTING TO THE START Pentewan lies just off the B3273, abut 1.5 miles (2.4km) north of Mevagissey. Lane-side parking in Pentewan is limited but there is a free car park.

THE PUB The Ship, Pentewan. Tel: 01726 842855; www.staustellbrewery.co.uk

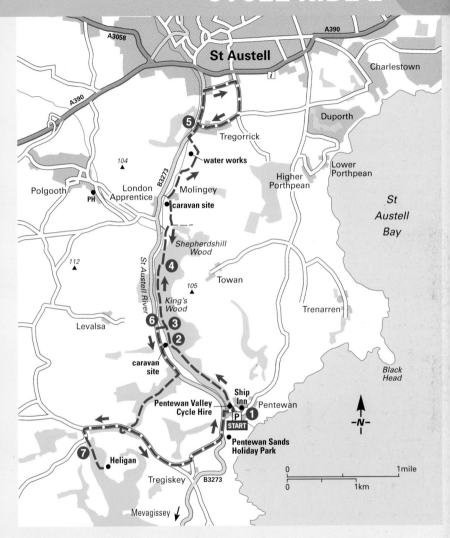

A3058

A390

A390

St Austell

Charlestown

B3273

Duporth

5

Tregorrick

● water works

104 ▲

London
Apprentice

Molingey

Polgooth

PH

● caravan site

Higher
Porthpean

Lower
Porthpean

*St
Austell
Bay*

St Austell River

*Shepherdshill
Wood*

4

105 ▲

Towan

Trenarren

112 ▲

*King's
Wood*

6 **3**

Levalsa

2

caravan
site

Black
Head

Ship
Inn

1

Pentewan

Pentewan Valley
Cycle Hire

P
START

● Pentewan Sands
Holiday Park

–N–

7

● Heligan

Tregiskey

B3273

0 _____ 1mile

0 _____ 1km

Mevagissey ↓

road. Bear left to reach a fork;
Mevagissey may be found via
the right fork. Keep left to
meet the road (note that this
road can be busy so please
take care); turn left for 0.5
mile (0.8km) to find Heligan
on the left.

7 On leaving Heligan, turn
right along the road. Cycle
gently downhill, with great
views over St Austell Bay.
Turn left on the first narrow
lane, steeply downhill. When
you meet the next minor road,
turn left, even more steeply,

to meet the B3273 opposite
Pentewan Sands Holiday
Park. Turn left towards the
Esso garage, then right into
Pentewan village.

REDRUTH MAP REF SW6942

Copper and tin mining created Redruth, and then abandoned it. Nevertheless, from the early 18th century until the middle of the 19th, Redruth was the true capital of Cornish mining. Redruth and the mining country that surrounds it, is now recognised for the importance of its industrial archaeology, and has been designated a World Heritage Site.

In the early days, the extraction method was tin-streaming, whereby tinners sifted through river sand and gravel for fragments of ore. The process caused disturbance, which released a red stain into rivers and streams and it was this that gave the town its name, although in odd reversal from what you would expect: red coming from 'rhyd' for ford, and 'ruth', meaning red.

The town contains some interesting buildings, including Georgian, Victorian neo-Gothic and art deco architecture. There is a great deal of brickwork and some startling features, such as the Italianate clock tower on the corner of Fore Street and Alma Place. Leading off Fore Street is Cross Street where there is a house with an external staircase, which was once the home of William Murdock, a Scottish engineer and inventor who worked in Redruth during the late 18th century. Among his many achievements, Murdock developed a lighting system using coal gas, and his home in Redruth was the first house in the world to be lit in this way (in 1872).

ROSELAND PENINSULA
MAP REF SW8536

This beautiful peninsula seems quietly detached from mainstream Cornwall. Flanked on its eastern side by a rock-fringed coast curving north into Gerrans Bay, it is bordered on the west by the River Fal, with Mylor and Feock set opposite. The very tip of the Roseland Peninsula is pierced by the twisting Percuil River that cuts deeply inland to create even smaller peninsulas. The area is famous for St Mawes, St Mawes Castle and for the Church of St Just-in-Roseland. A pleasant alternative to the A3078 onto the peninsula, is to take the A39 southwards from Truro, the B3289, past Trelissick Gardens and then cross the Fal by the King Harry Ferry. Another approach is to take the passenger ferry from Falmouth to St Mawes.

St Just-in-Roseland is an exquisite place. The church stands on the banks of a small creek, its mellow stonework embedded in a garden of shrubs and graceful trees that include palms as well as indigenous broad leaves.

■ Visit

CORNISH ENGINE HOUSES

North of Chapel Porth, standing on a lonely stretch of coastline, is the engine house of the Wheal Coates mine. It is one of many such distinctive buildings, which are a feature of the Cornish countryside, and once housed the engine that provided the essential services of winding, pumping and ventilation for the mine. Wheal Coates is an important relic of the county's industrial past, and has been restored by the National Trust, which cares for much of this historic coast. Chapel Porth lies at the heart of old mining country. The coast path to the south leads to Porthtowan.

On the promontory of land between Carrick Roads and the Percuil River stands St Mawes, deservedly popular and besieged with moored yachts in summer. On Castle Point to the west stands Henry VIII's St Mawes Castle, a quiet triumph of good Tudor design over function and renowned for its symmetry and decoration. The outer arm of the Roseland terminates at St Antony Head (one of the properties on the peninsula cared for by the National Trust) where there is a lighthouse and gun battery with an interesting history. On the east coast, further north, is Portscatho, open to the sea and with excellent sandy beaches nearby.

ST AGNES MAP REF SW7150

Mining made St Agnes. Tin and copper ore and lead from nearby mines were regularly exported from here by sea, but it was a difficult coast for sea-going. To either side of Trevaunance Cove below St Agnes the gaunt cliffs made landing by boat treacherous. Trevaunance had a small cramped harbour, where coal and other materials had to be raised by a winch-and-pulley system and the ore tipped down chutes. Since mining ceased in the early years of the last century, the sea has made a resort of this charming north coast village. Trevaunance Cove is quite small but it commands the seaward end of St Agnes. The village is easily accessible from the A30 yet seems pleasantly detached from a busier Cornwall. It is a convoluted village with a one-way system that may confuse you at first. A row of picturesque cottages, called Stippy Stappy, leads down from

the upper village to the valley below. There is a fine little local history museum in Penwinnick Road.

To the west lies St Agnes Beacon, reached by following Beacon Drive to a National Trust parking area on its north side. A good path leads easily to the summit and to spectacular views along the coast to north and south.

Just to the south of St Agnes is the sandy cove of Chapel Porth, while north of Chapel Porth, reached along the coast path, are the impressive remains of the Towanroath engine house, restored by the National Trust. Dating from 1872, it housed the massive steam engine used to pump water from the nearby Wheal Coates mine.

ST AUSTELL MAP REF SX0152

Cornwall's famous clay 'Alps' dominate the landscape around St Austell. The town is a good shopping centre, but its outlook is marred by the industrial sprawl that surrounds it – the price of vigorous industry. Even when it was a mere village St Austell was the centre of good farming country, open-cast tin extraction and stone quarrying. Today, the centre of St Austell has been largely modernised, to some extent in sympathy with its fine traditional buildings. Fore Street and the area around Holy Trinity have been conserved and the Town Hall is in bold Renaissance style, a granite palazzo incorporating a splendid market hall with its interior still intact. The Church of The Holy Trinity has sculpted figures set within niches in the tower, which itself is faced with Pentewan stone from the coastal quarries to the

■ Activity

CLAY COUNTRY CIRCUIT

The vast spoil tips of the St Austell clay country are composed of feldspar and quartz. The raw clay is stripped from the faces of the pits by high pressure hoses creating flooded pits, their translucent green and blue waters adding to the odd surrealism of this 'lunar' landscape. The best way to appreciate the clay country is to drive through it – explore the area north and west of St Austell between the B3279 and the B3274, which takes in Nanpean, Roche, the Roche Rock and China Clay Country Park at Carthew.

south. The pearly-grey stone has a warmer tinge when wet.

To the north of St Agnes, is Cornwall's most startling industrial landscape, from which clay has been extracted on a massive scale. The clay was once used for making porcelain but is now used mainly in paper-making.

About three million tonnes are produced in the St Austell area annually. Much waste is generated and the great snowy tips have created a strangely compelling landscape that now hosts the spectacular Eden Project with its futuristic biomes. The China Clay Country Park is situated at Carthew to the north of St Austell on the B3274. Further north again is the village of Roche with its adjacent Roche Rock. This remarkable outcrop of quartz schorl, an altered granite, is unique in Cornwall and a startling feature in the midst of the industrial landscape. The largest outcrop is crowned by the ruins of the chapel of St Michael, built in 1409.

ST COLUMB MAJOR
MAP REF SW9163

St Columb Major set on high ground 5 miles (8km) east of Newquay, was once traffic-bound but a bypass has eased the congestion in its narrow streets, which are enclosed between slate-hung houses. There is some very fine architecture, including an Italianate Gothic building of red and yellow bricks that now houses a bank. Opposite is the attractive Red Lion Inn, and much of the main square dates from the Regency period. The Church of St Columba has a procession arch through the base of its impressive tower.

TRELISSICK   MAP REF SX8339

Trelissick is a beautiful woodland park of some 370 acres (148ha), overlooking the Fal Estuary and owned by the National Trust; the house is not open to the public. The grounds were laid out with carriage drives and were planted with trees during the 1820s to take full advantage of the picturesque views. The parkland is criss-crossed with pathways, which provide some delightful walks.

In the garden's sheltered position many unusual and exotic plants thrive, including subtropical species from South America and Tasmania. But the gardens are particularly noted for their collection of camellias, magnolias and hydrangeas, of which there are more than 100 varieties. The large walled garden has fig trees and climbing plants, and there is a shrub garden. Plants are available in the garden shop and there is an art and craft gallery and a restaurant. Theatrical and musical events are often held here.

TRURO MAP REF SW8244

Truro's great cathedral catches the eye from all quarters. It rises from the heart of the city, its honey-coloured stone and lancet windows reflecting the sun, its great Gothic towers piercing the sky. There is no trace of the Norman castle that once stood at Truro, nor of the Dominican friary that stood near the low ground by the river, but the cathedral makes up for their loss.

Truro's fortunes rose and fell over the years, but by the late 18th century it had become the political and cultural centre of Georgian Cornwall. It was during the last years of the 18th century that such famous features as Boscawen Street and Lemon Street were built. Today Boscawen Street is a broad, cobbled space, entered at both ends from narrow thoroughfares. The granite façade of the City Hall graces Boscawen Street, and Lemon Street survives as one of the finest examples of a late Georgian street in Britain, its houses perfectly aligned to either side of a broad avenue that climbs uphill.

There are hidden glories in Truro amid the modern developments. From the Moorfield car park, a lane leads to Victoria Square, but parallel and to its right is the elegant Georgian crescent of Walsingham Place. Throughout the heart of Truro, the lanes connecting the main streets are lined with attractive shops, cafés and restaurants. From the west end of Boscawen Street, King Street leads up to the pedestrianised area of High Cross in front of the cathedral. The stylish Assembly Rooms, with a façade of Bath stone, stands nearby.

Seen from its forecourt the cathedral seems crowded in by buildings, instead of being the dominating presence that commands the view from outside the city. But the west front with its soaring towers is exhilarating. The foundation stones of the cathedral were laid in 1880 and the western towers were finally dedicated in 1920. Truro's cathedral is thus a Victorian building. It is Early English Gothic in design but with strong French influences that are seen in the great spires. The interior is glorious. It is vaulted throughout and pillars and arches are in elegant proportion, the air light beneath the great roofs. There are beautiful individual features such as the exquisite baptistry. All that remains of the old parish church of St Mary's is incorporated into the south aisle. Those with an eye for ancient stonework may find the outer wall of the old church a reassuring contrast to the smooth planes of the Victorian cathedral.

Pydar Street runs north from the cathedral as a pleasant pedestrian concourse. A short distance away is the stylish Crown Court, and below here are the pleasant Victoria Gardens. Boscawen Park, by the Truro River, is reached along the road to Malpas. The Royal Cornwall Museum in River Street has an excellent collection of minerals and there are exhibitions covering archaeology and mining. The art gallery has works by John Opie, the 18th-century portrait painter, who was born near St Agnes. Truro is an excellent shopping centre with numerous independent and specialist shops offering a great variety of quality goods.

■ TOURIST INFORMATION CENTRES

Mevagissey
St Georges Square.
Tel: 01726 844857; www.
mevagissey-cornwall.co.uk

Newquay
Municipal Buildings, Marcus
Hill. Tel: 01637 854020;
www.visitnewquay.org.uk

St Austell
Bypass Service Station,
Southbourne Road.
Tel: 01726 879500; www.
visitthecornishriviera.co.uk

Truro
Municipal Buildings,
Boscawen Street.
Tel: 01872 274555;
www.tourismtruro.gov.uk

■ PLACES OF INTEREST

Blue Reef Aquarium
Towan Promenade, Newquay.
Tel: 01637 878134;
www.bluereefaquarium.co.uk

Caerhays Castle and Gardens
Gorran, St Austell.
Tel: 01872 501310;
www.caerhays.co.uk

Carwinion Garden
Mawnan Smith,
Falmouth.
Tel: 01326 250258;
www.carwinion.co.uk

Charlestown Shipwreck and Heritage Centre
Charlestown,
near St Austell.
Tel: 01726 69897; www.
shipwreckcharlestown.com

China Clay Country Park
Wheal Martyn, Carthew,
St Austell. Tel: 01726 850362;
www.chinaclaycountry.co.uk

Cornish Mines and Engines
Pool, near Redruth.
Tel: 01209 315027

Cornish Cyder Farm
Penhallow, Truro.
Tel: 01872 573356; www.
thecornishcyderfarm.co.uk

The Eden Project
Bodelva, St Austell.
Tel: 01726 811911;
www.edenproject.com

Lost Gardens of Heligan
Pentewan, near Mevagissey.
Tel: 01726 845100;
www.heligan.com

Mevagissey Aquarium
South Quay.
Tel: 01726 843305

Polmassick Vineyard
St Ewe, near Mevagissey.
Tel: 01726 842239

Royal Cornwall Museum
River Street, Truro.
Tel: 01872 272205; www.
royalcornwallmuseum.org.uk

Trelissick Garden
Feock, near Truro.
Tel: 01872 862090

■ FOR CHILDREN

Cornish Birds of Prey Centre
Winnards Perch, St Columb
Major. Tel: 01637 880544;
www.cornishbirdsofprey.co.uk

Dairy Land Farm World
Tresillian Barton, Newquay.
Tel: 01872 510349

Holywell Bay Fun Park
Newquay.
Tel: 01637 830095;
www.holywellbay.co.uk

Lappa Valley Steam Railway
St Newlyn East, near
Newquay. Tel: 01872 510317;
www.lappavalley.co.uk

Newquay Zoo
Trenance Gardens, Newquay.
Tel: 01637 873342;
www.newquayzoo.org.uk

Screech Owl Sanctuary
Goss Moor, St Colomb.
Tel: 01726 860182;
www.screechowlsanctuary.
co.uk

World of Model Railways
Meadow Street, Mevagissey.
Tel: 01726 842457;
www.model-railway.co.uk

■ SHOPPING

Camborne
Large covered and open-air
market at Pool, Sat and Sun.

Newquay
Covered market daily.

Par
Large covered market at
Stadium Park, Sat, Sun, and
Wed in summer.

St Austell
Open market in town centre,
Fri and Sat.
Shopping precinct, Old
Market House.

Truro
Pannier Market. Mon–Sat.
Lemon Street Market.
Mon–Sat.

■ LOCAL SPECIALITIES

Crafts

Cornwall Crafts Association,
Trelissick Gardens, near
Truro. Tel: 01872 864514;
www.cornwallcrafts.co.uk
Mid Cornwall Galleries, St
Blazey Gate, near St Austell.
Tel: 01726 812131; www.
mid-cornwall-galleries.co.uk

■ SPORTS & ACTIVITIES

ANGLING

Sea

Mevagissey Shark Angling
Centre. Tel: 01726 843430
National Boatmen's
Association, Newquay.
Tel: 01637 876352; www.
newquay-harbour.com

Coarse

Porth Reservoir, near
Newquay. Tel: 01566 771930

BEACHES

*Lifeguards, where indicated,
are on summer service.
Dogs are not allowed on
several popular beaches from
Easter Day to 1st October.
During winter, when dogs are
allowed, owners must use
poop scoops.*

Crinnis Beach, Carlyon Bay

Long beach, very popular.

Crantock Beach

Backed by sand dunes.
Estuary dangerous for
swimming. Lifeguard.

Holywell Bay

Large sandy beach with
dunes, surfing. Lifeguard.

Newquay Watergate Bay

Large west-facing beach.
Can be breezy. Lifeguard.

Porth Beach

Safe bathing.

Lusty Glaze

Backed by cliffs. Lifeguard

Tolcarne Beach

Surfing. Lifeguard.

Towan Beach

Large sandy beach. Lifeguard

Great Western

Surfing beach. Lifeguard.

Fistral Beach

Large, popular, international
surfing venue. Lifeguard.

Perranporth Village Beach

Popular beach. Lifeguard.

Porthtowan

Large busy beach. Lifeguard.

Portreath

Popular north-facing beach.

Roseland Peninsula

Small beaches in St Mawes
and Portscatho.

St Agnes Trevaunance

Small, popular, reduced
during highest tides. Surfing.

Chapel Porth

Long stretch of sand, reduced
greatly at high tide. Surfing.
Lifeguard.

BOAT TRIPS

Mevagissey and Newquay

Booking offices at harbours.

Truro

River trips from Town Quay
or Malpas to Falmouth.
Enterprise Boats
Tel: 01326 374241/ 313234;
www.enterprise-boats.co.uk

■ COUNTRY PARKS & NATURE RESERVES

Tehidy Country Park

Near Camborne.
Tel: 01872 222000

CYCLE HIRE

Newquay

Cycle Revolution, 7 Beach
Road. Tel: 01637 872634

Mevagissey

Pentewan Valley Cycle Hire,
1 West End, Pentewan.
Tel: 01726 844242; www.
pentewanvalleycyclehire.co.uk

■ EVENTS & CUSTOMS

Camborne

Trevithick Day. Stalls,
dancing, steam engines,
Apr.

Charlestown

Regatta Week, late Jul.

Mevagissey

Mevagissey Feast Week, Jun.

Newquay

Cornwall Gardens Festival,
mid-Mar to May.
Run to the Sun Festival, May.
Pro-Am Surf Championships,
Aug.
Surf, Skate and Music
Festival, Aug.
British National Surf
Championships, Sep.
Championship Gig Racing,
Sep.
Newquay Fish Festival, Sep.
Newquay Music and Flower
Festival, Sep.

St Mawes

Town Regatta, Jul.

Lizard Peninsula

The Lizard Peninsula is a large area of downland fringed by sea cliffs of variegated serpentine and slate. The peninsula ends at Lizard Point, the most southerly point in Britain. Along its coastline, lovely beaches line the edge of coves and bays. The Lizard is famous for the rare plants that grow on its spacious heathland and on its coastal fringe. To the north of Lizard Point is the Helford River where a softer landscape of wooded creeks and quiet villages leads on to the great natural harbour of Falmouth. At the western gateway to the Lizard is the busy town of Helston.

7	Walk start point
2	Tour start point

THE LIGHTHOUSE, LIZARD POINT

Unmissable attractions

The Lizard Peninsula is less well-known than Land's End, yet its corrugated coastline of black cliffs and coves can seem even more dramatic. It is at its most beautiful at Kynance Cove and Mullion, where offshore islands of multicoloured serpentine rock echo to the calls of sea birds. Inland is Helston, a pleasant market town famous for its Flora Day Festival. Past Cadgwith and Coverack, Cornwall becomes leafy and green and there are superb opportunities for walks and cycles.

1 Falmouth
Busy with all types of vessels, Falmouth's harbour is backed by whitewashed cottages and lush green countryside.

2 National Seal Sanctuary
This centre, in the village of Gweek, near Helston, rescues and rehabilitates sick or abandoned seals before releasing them back into the wild.

3 Lizard Point
Visitors to the café at Lizard Point, England's most southerly point, enjoy far-reaching sea views. The area is renowned for its craggy cliff scenery, wooded vales and breezy windswept downs.

4 Mullion Cove
The small working harbour at Mullion is in the care of the National Trust. The boats here land mainly crabs, lobster and crawfish.

5 Helford Estuary
Pretty cottages nestle in the sheltered, tree-lined tidal creeks of the tranquil Helford Estuary.

6 Cadgwith
Fishing boats are drawn up onto the small beach in the tiny village of Cadgwith, which lies on the eastern side of the Lizard. Local fishermen fish daily for crab, lobster, shark, mullet and mackerel.

Around Cadgwith

A wandering route between coast and countryside through the serpentine rock landscape. These sinuous veins of green, red, yellow and white rock are a particular feature of the Lizard Peninsula. The walk leads inland to the sleepy village of Ruan from where a narrow lane leads down to the Poltesco Valley. From Carleon Cove the coast path is followed pleasantly to Cadgwith, an archetypal Cornish fishing village. Beyond the village, the coast path leads to the Devil's Frying Pan, a vast gulf in the cliffs caused by the collapse of a section of coast. From here the path leads on for a short distance along the edge of the cliffs before the route turns inland to the Church of the Holy Cross at Grade. Two fields beyond the church you will find the ancient St Ruan's Well and the road that leads back to the start of this ramble.

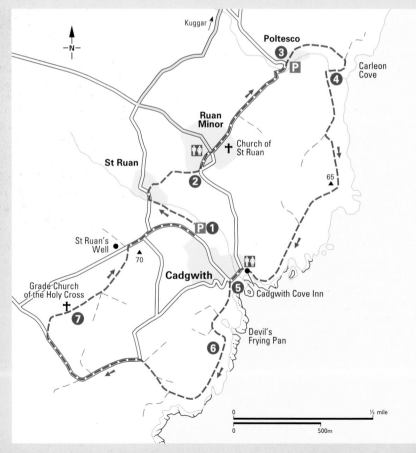

Route Directions

1 Go left along a grassy ride below the car park, to a stile. Continue through a gate and into woodland. Turn right at a lane, then on the corner, go up a track and continue to the main road at Ruan Minor.

2 Go left and, just beyond the shop, turn left down a surfaced path. Rejoin the main road by a thatched cottage (there are toilets just before the road). Cross diagonally right, then go down a lane past the Church of St Ruan.

3 In 0.3 mile (500m), just past an old mill and a bridge, go right at a T-junction to reach the car park at Poltesco. From the far end of the car park follow a track, signposted 'Carleon Cove'. Go right at a junction.

4 Go over a wooden bridge above the cove, then turn left at a T-junction and again turn left in 0.25 mile (400m) where the path branches. Go through a kissing gate and continue along the cliff-edge path to Cadgwith. At the road, turn left.

5 Follow a narrow path, signposted 'Coast Path'. By a house gateway, go left up a surfaced path, signposted 'Devil's Frying Pan'. At an open area turn left, pass Townplace Cottage, cross a meadow and reach the Devil's Frying Pan itself.

6 Keep on the coast path and at a junction, just past a chalet studio, follow a path inland to a T-junction with a rough track. Turn left and then, at a public lane, go left again and after 0.5 mile (800m) turn right along a track to Grade Church.

7 Follow the left-hand field-edge behind the church, then go over a stile into the next field to reach a lane. St Ruan's Well is opposite diagonally left. Turn right for 200yds (183m), then branch off right between stone pillars to return to the car park.

Route facts

DISTANCE/TIME 4.5 miles (7.2km) 3h

MAP OS Explorer 103 The Lizard

START Cadgwith car park, about 350 yards (320m) from Cadgwith. Busy in summer; grid ref: SW 720146

TRACKS Very good, coast path occasionally rocky in places, field paths

GETTING TO THE START
From the A394 at Helston take the A3083 south, signposted 'The Lizard'. After 8 miles (12.9km) turn left for Cadgwith and follow signs for the car park. Avoid entering the village as the lanes are very steep and narrow.

THE PUB Cadgwith Cove Inn, Cadgwith Cove. Tel: 01326 290513; www.cadgwithcoveinn.com

❶ There are two moderate climbs along the coast paths and the cliff path can be slippery when wet.

FALMOUTH MAP REF SW8032

Vessels of all types and sizes still bustle in and out of Falmouth harbour, lending excitement and atmosphere to one of the world's largest natural harbours. Falmouth developed as a port after Henry VIII built Pendennis and St Mawes castles, the guardians of the Fal Estuary. Both are built in the distinctive clover-leaf design and St Mawes is particularly renowned as a fine example of military architecture. Visitors here can explore the dungeons, barrack rooms and cannon-lined castle walls.

During the late 17th century the port became a packet station, from where small, fast-sailing brigantines took mail to northwest Spain, and in later years to North America, the West Indies and South America. Gold and silver bullion was carried and the packets provided a passenger service. By the 1830s over 40 packets worked out of Falmouth. They were well-armed against privateers, French naval hostility and even Algerian pirates. The crews supplemented their meagre wages with smuggling and by carrying unofficial goods; there are rich tales of villainy and swashbuckling. The packet service had transferred to Southampton by 1850 but Falmouth's position as a major port was secured by a vigorous pilchard fishery, the development of Falmouth docks and a thriving shipbuilding industry. Ship repair, bunkering, cargo handling and yacht building are local industries that continue today.

Falmouth's rather straggling form gives it less unity than might be expected of a port, as the town follows the riverside through a chain of linking main streets, but this makes it intriguing to explore. It is centred on The Moor, once just a muddy creek and now emphatically urban, and it is here that you will find the Falmouth Art Gallery, well worth a visit, on the upper floor of the old Passmore Edwards Free Library. As well as changing exhibitions there are permanent displays of paintings including those of Henry Scott Tuke, the Victorian painter who spent his last years near Falmouth. From The Moor, Webber Street leads to the Prince of Wales Pier. Market Street is the first of Falmouth's long chain of streets that leads along the riverfront. The walk along Market Street, Church Street and Arwenack Street should be varied by diversions to the town quays from where there are panoramic views across the river mouth.

Some of Falmouth's many engaging features include the 111-step Jacob's

■ Activity

FALMOUTH AFLOAT

Various river and sea cruises are available from Falmouth's Prince of Wales Pier and from other boarding points around the estuary. Ferries leave for Flushing and St Mawes, and when the tide allows, there are cruises upriver to Malpas, from where a five-minute bus ride connects with Truro. An enjoyable trip can be made upriver to Tolverne on the Roseland Peninsula. If you are confident of having good sea legs, there are trips along the coast and then up the Helford River; evening cruises on the Fal are another option along with sea-angling trips from the Prince of Wales Pier.

Ladder that leads up from The Moor, and watch out for the recurring theme of Falmouth's 'Opes', the passageways, which run between the town's buildings.

Pendennis Castle is located on the headland to the east of Falmouth and is easily reached from the waterfront. Of the several very pleasant beaches along Falmouth's southern seafront, Gyllyngvase is the largest and most popular. The National Maritime Museum Cornwall, on Falmouth's waterfront, includes the National Small Boat Collection of 120 boats. Various craft are also moored alongside the museum's pontoon from where they are regularly sailed. Cornwall's maritime heritage is portrayed through reconstructions, special exhibitions, exciting audio-visual and interactive displays, which includes hands-on operation of model boats, and there are live demonstrations of boat construction. There is also a unique tidal gallery with windows that reveal the rise and fall of the tide, and breathtaking views across Falmouth Harbour from a 95-foot (29m) tower.

Use the Park & Float in summer and sail to the museum in a classic ferry.

GUNWALLOE MAP REF SW6522

The road to Gunwalloe ends at Church Cove where an intriguing little 15th-century church nestles close to the edge of eroded cliffs. The cliffs have been stabilised by huge rocks to create a breakwater. North of the church is the noisily named Jangye-ryn Cove. Inland lie extensive sand dunes; a golf course crowns the green swell of the higher land in rather odd counterpoint.

■ Visit

LIZARD LAKES
Cornwall has few natural lakes of any size but there are reservoirs that make a pleasant change from the sea. The Argal and College Waterpark is only about 2 miles (3km) from Falmouth along the A394. The reservoir here is tree-fringed and very peaceful, with much birdlife and pleasant paths skirting the shoreline. Coarse fishing is available all year and the fly-fishing season is from March to October. Stithians Lake is within easy reach of Falmouth and Helston along the A394. There is a carpark on the east side of the lake near the dam and another at its north end, near the watersports centre.

The coastline is often lively, as it is west facing and open to boisterous seas. Shipwrecks were common during the days of sail when vessels became trapped within the horns of Mount's Bay; the price of not giving the Lizard a wide enough berth was grief on Gunwalloe's shoreline. The name of Dollar Cove below the church reflects the loss of a Spanish treasure ship in the 1780s.

Halzephron Cove and Gunwalloe Fishing Cove lie just north of Church Cove and can be reached along the coast path. The National Trust has solved the problem of scattered parking at Gunwalloe with a screened car park on the approach to Church Cove. Though the problem of sea erosion is another matter. The sea is threatening to break through the neck of land between Dollar Cove and Church Cove and large blocks of granite have been tipped onto the beach to break the force of the waves.

Helford River and The Lizard

An absorbing drive past some lovely lakes and on through the popular Helford River area with its quiet tidal creeks to The Lizard, Britain's most southerly point.

Route Directions

The tour starts in Helston, once a port and then an important trading centre.

1 Leave Helston on B3297, signed 'Redruth'. After 6 miles (9.6km), having passed via Wendron and the access to Poldark Mine, turn right on to an unclassified road, signed 'Carnmenellis'. After 2 miles (3.2km), at a T-junction turn left, signed 'Stithians'. Continue ahead, with Stithians Reservoir on the right.
The reservoir is noted as a good watersports centre and for its superior birdlife (so remember to take your binoculars with you).

2 Pass the Golden Lion Inn and continue across a causeway. At the next junction turn right, signed 'Stithians', and continue through Goonlaze. (Note: access road to Stithians dam and car park, just after Goonlaze). Continue through Stithians (toilets just past the church), then, on the other side of the village at a crossroads, go straight across and down Tregonning Road, signed 'Mabe'. Follow a very

narrow lane for 1.25 miles (2km) then go right at a T-junction, signed 'Longdowns'. In 0.75 miles (1.2km), just after a quarry, go left at a T-junction. Soon, reach the A394 and turn left, signed 'Falmouth'. A short distance ahead, and just past a garage, branch right. Reach Mabe Burnthouse and, at a junction at the village centre, bear right, signed 'Mawnan' and 'Constantine'. Keep left at the next junction, signed 'Mawnan Smith'.
A short distance further on, a side road branches right to Argal & College Water Park (toilets). There is a car parking area and there are several waterside walks.

3 On the main route, follow signs for Mawnan Smith. Go directly over a crossroads, signed 'Mawnan Smith and Helford Passage' and continue for 2 miles (3.2km) to reach Mawnan Smith, a pleasant village within lovely surroundings. Keep right by the Red Lion Inn, signed 'Budock Vean', and follow signs for Helford Passage and Constantine. Continue,

passing Glendurgan Garden, a woodland valley garden of 40 acres (16ha), then pass the equally fine Trebah Gardens. The gardens are filled with subtropical plants in an area of more than 25 acres (10ha) with plenty to amuse children and interest adults. Careful planting has ensured year-round colour.

4 Follow signs for Porth Navas and Constantine along a winding and often narrow lane (with passing places). Pass through Porth Navas and follow the signs for Constantine. When you reach a T-junction, go left through Constantine. On the far side of the village ignore the first left turn signed 'Vicarage Terrace, Gweek' and take the next left turn signed 'Gweek'. Pass through Brill and turn left at the next junction signed 'Gweek'. Go through Gweek. (Just past the Gweek Inn and before a bridge, a road to the left, called 'Meneth', leads to the National Seal Sanctuary.) Gweek, just beyond Culdrose, is the home of the National Seal Sanctuary, Europe's largest rescue centre for seals. Injured seal pups are diligently cared for at the hospital and returned to the sea when they are fit and healthy. Those that are too badly disabled are given a new home at the sanctuary.

5 Go left by a thatched house, signed 'Mawgan' and 'St Keverne'. Continue through a wooded area and, at a roundabout, go left, signed 'Mawgan'. Drive carefully through Mawgan, keeping left at a junction, signed 'Manaccan and Helford', pass Mawgan church and then follow signs for Manaccan and Helford along a narrow and winding road with some steep inclines and sharp bends. Pass through St Martin and reach Newtown-in-St Martin. The main route goes right at a junction, just past the Prince of Wales pub. (For a diversion to Helford, keep past this junction to reach a junction with a road leading left signed 'Manaccan, Helford'.) On the main route, continue onwards to a junction with the B3293. Turn left, signed 'St Keverne'. Pass the Goonhilly Satellite Earth Station.
Goonhilly is a complex of giant communication antennas.

6 A few hundred yards beyond the Earth Station turn right, signed 'Cadgwith and

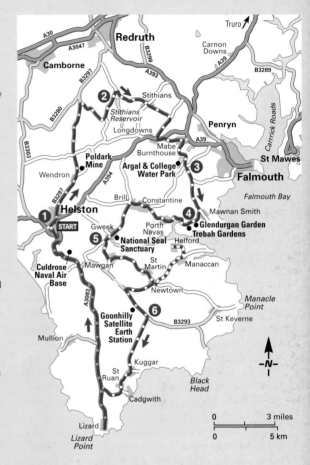

Kennack Sands', and follow an arrow-straight road to reach Kuggar. At a junction, turn right signed 'The Lizard'. At the next crossroads go forward, signed 'St Ruan and Cadgwith'. Continue through St Ruan and after about half a mile (0.8km) pass a side road leading left. (300 yards/274m

down this side road is large car park for Cadgwith.) On the main route keep ahead, and continue following signs for The Lizard. At a junction with the A3083, turn left for Lizard Point (toilets). Return along the A3083 to Helston, passing Culdrose Naval Air Station on the way back to Helford.

The coast path leads west above high cliffs. To the east it passes through a green, sheltered landscape above cliffs draped with the invasive Hottentot Fig, or *mesembryanthemum*. The Lizard's position, jutting out into the Channel approaches, has made it dangerous to vessels. For a mile (1.6km) seaward off Lizard Point the sea tumbles in frightening overfalls during stormy weather. To the northeast lies the blunt promontory of Black Head and beyond here the deadly Manacles Reef.

The fortress-like Lizard Lighthouse dominates the coast to the east. A warning light was first established here in 1612. Today's powerful light flashes every three seconds and can be seen in clear weather from up to 29 miles (46.7km) away. The fog signal is delivered by siren every 60 seconds.

About 1.5 miles (2.4km) east of Lizard Point is Church Cove, and its attractive little church of Landewednack. The cove is reached on foot from the car park past thatched cottages. A short walk south along the coast path leads to the remarkable cliffside site of the Lizard-Cadgwith lifeboat house.

MULLION MAP REF SW6719
Mullion is a large village a short distance inland from the harbour at Mullion Cove. There is a nice sense of anticipation on first approaching Mullion and the village lives up to expectations – a bustling place with an excellent variety of shops, art and craft galleries and good pubs. The Church of St Melanus has a remarkable collection of bench-ends depicting characters, including a jester and a monk. Mullion Cove is fascinating. Big cliffs and sea stacks, gold-leafed with yellow lichen, enclose the narrow inlet and its substantial piers. Offshore lies the bulky mass of Mullion Island, flickering with seabirds.

The coast to the south is pleasantly remote, especially around Predannack Head and Vellan Head, with delightful coast walks to either side of the cove. Just to the north of Mullion is Polurrian Cove where there is a large sandy beach and further north again is the popular Poldhu Cove with its sandy dunes.

PORTHLEVEN MAP REF SW6225
Porthleven was noted for its shipbuilding and fishing industries. Remarkably, both have survived and the village remains a truly Cornish place. The centrepiece inner harbour is lined along its quays with an interesting mix of galleries, shops, pubs, restaurants and cafés. On the north side of the outer harbour is a wave-cut platform of deeply pocketed and riven slate where a huge boulder, the Giant's Rock, is exposed at low tide. It is believed to be a glacial 'erratic' carried here probably embedded in an ice floe during the last Ice Age.

Victorian villas on the South Quay create a pleasing background to the harbour road and bustling quayside. To the southeast, a road lined with cottages leads along the cliff edge and Loe Bar Road, leads to a car park, for the short walk to Loe Bar and the Penrose estate.

Be warned that Porthleven harbour is very vulnerable to high tides and you should never walk along the outer piers. Swimming in this area is dangerous.

■ TOURIST INFORMATION CENTRES

Falmouth
11 Market Strand, Prince of Wales Pier. Tel: 01326 312300; www.discoverfalmouth.co.uk
Helston
79 Meneage Street.
Tel: 01326 565431
Lizard
www.visitlizardcornwall.co.uk

■ PLACES OF INTEREST

Falmouth Art Gallery
Municipal Buildings, The Moor. Tel: 01326 313863; www.falmouthartgallery.com Free.
Gardens
In addition to the larger gardens listed in this section, there are a number of smaller gardens open to the public, notably Carwinion at Mawnan Smith, Potager Garden at Constantine, and Bonython Manor near Cury Cross Lanes.
Tel: 01872 322900; www.gardensofcornwall.com
Glendurgan Garden
Mawnan Smith, near Falmouth. Tel: 01326 252020
Godolphin House
Godolphin Cross, Breage.
Tel: 01736 763194; www.godolphinhouse.com
Helston Folk Museum
Old Butter Market, Church Street.
Tel: 01326 564027. Free.

National Maritime Museum Cornwall
Discovery Quay, Falmouth.
Tel: 01326 313388; www.nmmc.co.uk
National Seal Sanctuary
Gweek.
Tel: 01326 221361; www.sealsanctuary.co.uk
Pendennis Castle
Falmouth.
Tel: 01326 316594.
Penjerrick Garden
Budock, Falmouth.
Tel: 01872 870105; www.penjerrickgarden.co.uk
Poldark Mine
Wendron, near Helston.
Tel: 01326 573173; www.poldark-mine.co.uk
Trebah Gardens
Mawnan Smith, near Falmouth.
Tel: 01326 252200; www.trebahgarden.co.uk
Trelowarren
Mawgan, Helston.
Tel: 01326 221224; www.trelowarren.co.uk
Trevarno Estate
Crowntown, Helston.
Tel: 01326 574274; www.trevarno.co.uk

■ FOR CHILDREN

The Flambards Experience
Helston.
Tel: 01326 573404; www.flambards.co.uk

■ SHOPPING

Falmouth
High Street, Market Street and Church Street.
Helston
Market Coinagehall Street, Mon and Sat.

■ LOCAL SPECIALITIES

CRAFTS
Beside The Wave
10 Arwenack Street, Falmouth.
Tel: 01326 211132; www.beside-the-wave.co.uk
Creftow Gallery & Studios
6 Church Street, Helston.
Tel: 01326 572848; www.creftow.com
Trelowarren Gallery,
Helston.
Tel: 01326 221224
Nic Harrison Ceramics
Penhale Jakes, Ashton, Helston.
Tel: 01326 762638; www.nicharrison.com
Trecarne Pottery
Meaver Road, Mullion.
Tel: 01326 241294; www.trecarnepottery.co.uk

■ PERFORMING ARTS

Princess Pavilion
Melvill Road, Falmouth.
Tel: 01326 211222

■ SPORTS & ACTIVITIES

ANGLING
Sea
Falmouth, Mullion, Cadgwith.

Coarse

Argal Reservoir, Penryn, Falmouth.
Tel: 01209 860301
Stithians Lake, Redruth.
Tel: 01209 860301

BEACHES

Lifeguards, where indicated, are on summer service. Dogs are not allowed on several popular beaches from Easter Day to 1st October. During winter, when dogs are allowed, owners must use poop scoops.

Falmouth

Swanpool: sandy with facilities nearby;
Gyllngvase: large, popular, family beach, safe bathing.
Church Cove: popular, sandy cove.

Kennack Sands

Large sandy beach, with numerous rock pools.

Kynance Cove

Steep beach at low tide. Steep steps to the beach.

Maenporth

Sheltered with level access.

Poldhu Cove

Near Mullion. Popular beach with dunes. Lifeguard.

Praa Sands

Huge beach popular with families and surfers. Lifeguard.

BOAT TRIPS

Falmouth

Prince of Wales Pier. Regular passenger ferries to St Mawes and Flushing. River cruises to Roseland Peninsula and Truro. Sea cruises.
www.enterprise-boats.co.uk

BOWLING

Falmouth Bowling Club, Tregenver Road.
Tel: 01326 315085; www. falmouthbowlingclub.co.uk

CYCLING

A network of quiet lanes offers good cycling between the main roads and main centres. Cycling is not permitted on public footpaths or on the coast path.

CYCLE HIRE

Helston

Family Cycles,
7 Church Street.
Tel: 01326 573719

GOLF COURSES

Falmouth

Falmouth Golf Club, Swanpool Road.
Tel: 01326 311262; www. falmouthgolfclub.com

Helston

Helston Golf and Leisure.
Tel: 01326 565103

Mawnan Smith

Budock Vean Golf and Country Club.
Tel: 01326 252100;
www.budockvean.co.uk

Mullion

Mullion Golf Club, Cury.
Tel: 01326 240685; www. mulliongolfclub.co.uk

HORSE-RIDING

Mullion

Newton Equestrian Centre.
Tel: 01326 240388; www. newton-equestrian.co.uk

SAILING

Mylor

Mylor Sailing School, Mylor Harbour. Tel: 01326 377633;
www.mylorsailingschool. co.uk

WATERSPORTS

Coverack

Coverack Windsurfing Centre.
Tel: 01326 280939;
www.coverack.co.uk

Stithians Lake

Between Falmouth and Helston off the A394.
Tel: 01209 860301;
www.swlakestrust.co.uk

■ **EVENTS & CUSTOMS**

Gig racing is a major sport in Cornwall. Races are held in the summer at such venues as Cadgwith and Porthleven.

Falmouth

Falmouth Regatta Week, Aug. Maritime events including racing of Falmouth classic yachts as well as dinghies.
www.falmouthweek.co.uk

Helston

Helston Flora Day, 8 May, or previous Sat if 8 May is a Sun or Mon. The famous Furry Dance is performed throughout the day starting at 7am. Market stalls.
www.helstonfloraday.co.uk

Tea Rooms

Miss Peapod's Kitchen Café

Jubilee Wharf, Penryn TR10 8FG. Tel: 01326 374424; www.misspeapod.co.uk

An eco-eaterie within Jubilee Wharf on Penryn's revitalised waterfront. The river views from the alfresco decking and the food are the stars, with excellent breakfasts, coffee and cakes and delicious lunches prepared from local produce, including organic meats from Rosuick Farm.

Polpeor Café

Lizard Point, The Lizard TR12 7HJ. Tel: 01326 290939

At Britain's most southerly café, perched high on the cliffs on Lizard Point, you can watch waves crashing onto rocks and choughs wheeling around the cliffs while you tuck into a local crab salad and sandwiches or a traditional cream tea. On fine summer days, the suntrap terrace right on the cliff edge is the place to eat.

Roskilly's Croust House

Tregellast Barton Farm, St Keverne, Helston TR12 8NX Tel: 01326 280479; www.roskillys.co.uk

Roskilly's is a family-run, working organic farm where they make one of Cornwall's much-loved ice creams, as well as clotted cream, fudge, preserves, jams and juices. A great family day out on the farm can culminate with a home-made lunch, tea and cake, or a delicious cream tea with warm scones and their famous clotted cream and fruity jams. All can be washed down with apple juice or cider made on the farm.

Pubs

Shipwrights Arms

Helford, Helston TR12 6JX Tel: 01326 231235

Stunningly located on the banks of the Helford Estuary, the narrow approach road is restricted to pedestrians only. This is a pretty thatched pub with a terraced garden and picnic benches on the water's edge. The bar is traditional, with rustic furnishings and plenty of nautical bits and pieces.

Cadgwith Cove Inn

Cadgwith, Ruan Minor, Helston TR12 7JX Tel: 01326 290513; www.cadgwithcoveinn.com

An unspoiled hamlet of thatched cottages is the setting for this old-fashioned, bustling local. Crab sandwiches and a pint of Sharp's Doom Bar provide the perfect lunch, best enjoyed on the sunny terrace with views across the cove.

Halzephron Inn

Gunwalloe, Helston TR12 7QB. Tel: 01326 240406; www.halzephron-inn.co.uk

The 500-year-old Halzephron Inn commands an enviable position perched high above Gunwalloe Cove. There's a warm welcome inside the two low-ceilinged bars and bistro-style restaurant. Expect to find local ales on handpump, and menus that utilise the best local ingredients. Arrive early for seafood chowder, cod in beer batter, or chargrilled beef with Madeira sauce.

The Ship

Porthleven, Helston TR13 9JS Tel: 01326 564204; www.theshipincornwall.co.uk

This old fisherman's pub enjoys a magnificent position looking across the harbour. The view is best appreciated from the terraced lawns behind the pub. On winter days, climb the flight of steps and take in the view from the warmth of a window seat in the bar. Here, quaff tip-top Sharp's beers and refuel on hearty pub food, perhaps monkfish in bacon or chargrilled lamb steak.

Land's End Peninsula

Cornwall's 'First and Last' peninsula is a vivid, atmospheric landscape of spectacular cliffs and golden beaches that are washed by the clear Atlantic waters. Inland, small fields and narrow, twisting lanes lie embedded within a network of granite hedges that are smothered with wild flowers. Prehistoric monuments stand amid the heather and pale grass of the moorland hills and the rugged Levant north coast is noted for the industrial archaeology of its abandoned tin mines.

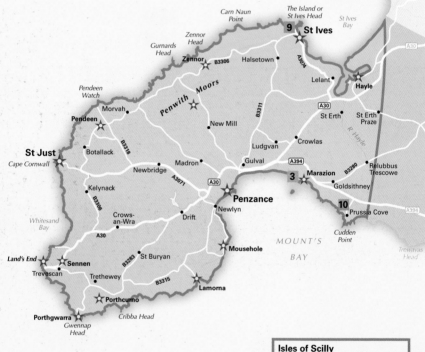

9 Walk start point

3 Cycle start point

NB Inset at 50% of mainland scale

LAND'S END

HAYLE BEACH

Unmissable attractions

The 'almost island' of the Lands End Peninsula seems like a bigger version of one of the Isles of Scilly. It is a world of spectacular promontories such as Gurnard's Head and Logan Rock, and its moorland hills. It is also a land of prehistoric stone circles and burial chambers. On the north coast is the resort of St Ives, the archetypal Cornish fishing village, where fishing and tourism happily co-exist. On the sunny south coast is Penzance at the heart of Mount's Bay with its island castle of St Michael's Mount. The peninsula has the ideal conditions for sailing, surfing and rock-climbing and the quieter pursuits of painting, birding and sea-fishing.

4

1 Tate St Ives
Overlooking Porthneor Beach, Tate St Ives exhibits the very best of Cornish contemporary art. Many of the works of art on display depict the extraordinary light that is found in and around St Ives.

2 Porthcurno Beach
Porthcurno completes the idyll with its glorious golden beach. Famed for its granite cliffs and sea of Mediterranean blue. Porthcurno Valley is also known for its historic telecommunications links. Visit the Telegraph Museum located just above Porthcurno car park.

3 Zennor
The dramatic coastal path near Zennor follows a succession of rugged points and headlands above high weathered granite cliffs. Below, are hidden sandy coves and clear blue sea.

4 Rock climbing, Zennor
Cornwall's challenging granite sea cliffs around Zennor are popular with rock climbers.

5 Mousehole
On the western edge of Mount's Bay, Mousehole's houses and cottages, linked by narrow alleyways, crouch above the high-walled little harbour that once sheltered a prosperous pilchard-fishing fleet.

5

HAYLE MAP REF SW5537

Hayle's industrial past was sustained by Victorian tin and copper mining, a fact reflected in local names such as Copperhouse and Foundry. Unfortunately, it is Hayle's rather straggling extent and its general decline that have denied it picturesque appeal; but awareness of the town's industrial past makes a visit rewarding for those looking for the history under the skin. A brisk walk along the eastern side of the harbour and along the northern side of the large tidal pond, Copperhouse Pool, though not entirely scenic, is worthwhile. The contrast between the dereliction of Hayle's harbour area and the spaciousness and brightness of its nearby beaches is quite startling. Access to several miles of golden beach, popular with families, sunbathers and surfers, can be gained from Hayle by following the road through the village of Phillack and out to a car park amid shoals of chalets. The town has a choice of shops, galleries and craft shops, restaurants and several down-to-earth pubs.

■ Activity

BIRDS OF A FEATHER

Hayle Estuary is an important winter feeding ground for wild birds, a bonus to birders in spring and autumn especially. Some very rare sightings are possible during autumn migrations when vagrant species from America may be pushed off their north-to-south migratory path and driven across the Atlantic to Cornwall. The best site is at Lelant Saltings to the west of Hayle. Access is from just off the A30 on the Penzance and St Ives road by the Old Quay House Inn.

LAMORNA MAP REF SW4424

Lamorna is the most sheltered of the narrow valleys that lead gently down to the south-facing shores of Mount's Bay. The road that leads down to Lamorna Valley is narrow and can become congested during Bank Holidays. It is a delightful road, nonetheless, descending through shady woodland to reach an unexpected bay that is fringed by granite cliffs. This is Lamorna's theme; there is charm around every corner if you are just willing to explore. Granite from Lamorna's hillside quarries was used to build many Victorian lighthouses and such famous features as the Thames Embankment. On the way down to the cove is the Wink Inn, a classic Cornish pub with an engaging atmosphere. The 'wink' signifies the blind eye that the gentry and local vicars often turned to old-time smuggling. Lamorna's rugged granite quay is a pleasant place to linger.

A mile (1.6km) west of Lamorna Valley in a field alongside the B3315 is a stone circle dating from the early Bronze Age – the famous Rosemodress, or Boleigh Circle of 19 upright stones. It is popularly known as the Merry Maidens, from entertaining but ridiculous legends of young girls turned to stone for dancing on a Sunday. In nearby fields are two tall standing stones, the Pipers, who suffered the same fate. They are all more likely to have been ceremonial sites of the Bronze Age peoples. A short distance west of the Merry Maidens, and close to the road, is the Tregiffian entrance grave. Also from the Bronze Age, it comprises a kerbed cairn with a chamber roofed with slabs.

LAND'S END   MAP REF SW3425

The symbolic geography of Land's End demands a visit, although the natural attractions of the area are perhaps best enjoyed outside the busiest holiday periods. Do not expect to find yourselves romantically alone during daylight hours – except in a Force 9 gale.

But while rugged weather may enhance the Land's End experience for the true romantic, the venue's numerous covered attractions are enjoyable as wet-weather alternatives. They include gift shops, craft centres and galleries, and some interesting exhibitions, including an interactive exhibition celebrating Britain's fascinating coastline, with touch-screen displays and a cliff-cam. There is a good choice of eating places within the complex and the Land's End Hotel is in a splendid position overlooking the Longships Lighthouse. There may be queues on the approach on popular Bank Holidays and during peak holiday periods.

Open access on foot, of course, is time-honoured and for those who prefer a more robust approach than by car, the coast path can be followed to Land's End from Sennen in the north (1 mile/1.6km) or from Porthgwarra in the southeast (3 miles/4.8km).

MARAZION   MAP REF SW5130

Marazion is a town first and foremost. You may earn yourself a deservedly frosty glance if you call this ancient borough anything less. It was the main trading port of Mount's Bay until an upstart Penzance developed its own markets and port during the 16th century. But

■ Insight

END-TO-ENDERS

The long walk from John O'Groats, at the northern tip of Scotland, to Land's End has attracted a multitude of people eager to cover the 603 miles (970km) in one piece. Famous End-to-Enders include Ian Botham and Jimmy Savile. Some began anonymously and then became famous, like the round-the-world walker Ffyona Campbell. Most make the trip for personal reasons, or for charities, which have benefited hugely from such efforts. There is even an official End-to-Enders Club. Straightforward walking remains the obvious challenge, but there have been numerous variations from four wheels to two wheels, bed-pushes, to nude cyclists (but only for the last few sunny Cornish miles). A few determined souls have done it via the coast.

Marazion has remained as distinctive as its lovely name, which derives, rather plainly, from the Cornish word for market. There is an informative little museum at the town hall in Market Square, antique and craft shops to browse and pleasant pubs, restaurants and cafés.

Marazion Beach offers safe bathing and is a glorious suntrap. It offers good windsurfing especially during spring and autumn, when conditions are breezy. The quiet village of Perranuthnoe, a short distance southeast with a south-facing beach also provides reasonable surfing at times. A few miles further east lies Prussia Cove, a secluded rocky inlet of great charm reached most rewardingly by a pleasant 2-mile (3.2km) walk along the coast path.

The great complement to Marazion is the castellated Isle of St Michael's Mount (cared for by the National Trust), the most romantic offshore island in Britain and a matching image to Mont St Michel off the Normandy coast. The Mount was dedicated to St Michael after claims of miraculous sightings of the saint by 5th-century fishermen. Even today shafts of celestial light seem drawn to St Michael's Mount although a view of angels is perhaps less likely. In its day the Mount has been monastery, prison, and castle-under-siege. The Mount is nicely defined as a part-time island by successive high tides during which it may be reached by a pleasant boat trip. At low tide the approach is on foot along a fine cobbled causeway.

MOUSEHOLE   MAP REF SW4626

Quaintness clings to Mousehole's name like a cat. But 'Mouz'l', as it should be pronounced, is a fishing village of strong character, though the days are long gone when its harbour was crammed with pilchard-fishing boats. The name derives from obscure roots. Its old Cornish name is Porth Enys, meaning 'the landing place by the island'. The small island offshore from Mousehole is called St Clement's after a hermit who is said to have maintained a warning light.

Tempting alleyways and passages wriggle between sturdy cottages in Mousehole and the harbourside Ship Inn rounds things off with a flourish. The far end of Mousehole's tiny harbour has a splendid inner wall of irregular granite blocks, a perfect subject for imaginative photography or sketching. There are some shops, including craft shops, cafés and restaurants. Mousehole was not built for the motor car and is best explored on foot. There is a car park by the harbour but it fills quickly during busy periods. The other is just outside the village on the road from Newlyn.

A steep hill leads inland from Mousehole to the village of Paul where the Church of St Pol de Leon has some impressive features. These include a memorial to the Mousehole crew of the local lifeboat, the *Solomon Browne*. They died heroically near Lamorna during an appalling storm in December 1981 after repeated attempts to save the eight people aboard the wrecked cargo vessel *Union Star*. The road out of Mousehole to the west leads up the dauntingly steep Raginnis Hill. Part way up is the famous Mousehole Bird Hospital, a refuge for countless injured birds many of which are the victims of oil pollution. The recovery cages often contain several very vocal birds.

■ Insight

DISHY FISH

Pilchards are not so easy to come by these days, but a good Cornish fish merchant will have a splendid selection of fish to tempt you. Mackerel are a good fleshy fish, though oily; the old Cornish treatment was to 'souse' them in vinegar and bay leaves, but today smoked and peppered mackerel are available. And very tasty, too. Hake, cod, haddock and ling are all meaty, flavoursome fish. Best of all are John Dory and turbot. Expensive Dover and lemon sole will tempt the taste, but test the treasury. Monkfish is good for imaginative cooking. Bon appetit!

Marazion to Penzance

Enjoy an easy ride along one of south Cornwall's most beautiful bays. This level, easy, there-and-back route along the edge of Mount's Bay, with spectacular views over St Michael's Mount, is an ideal option for families with young children. With just a short road stretch at the start and finish, the ride runs along the back of the huge expanse of sands between Marazion and Penzance.

Route Directions

1 This ride is part of the First and Last Trail, the first stretch of the Cornish Way long-distance cycle route, which starts at Land's End and runs for 180 miles (288km) through the county. Marazion, where this ride starts, is Cornwall's oldest charter town, dating from 1257. Its unusual name comes from the Cornish 'marghas yow' – meaning 'Thursday market'. Marazion was the main trading port in Mount's Bay until Penzance overtook it in the 16th century. It's worth having a look around this attractive village before you set off. From the pub car park cycle uphill (away from the beach) onto West End. (The Godolphin Arms can be found by turning right.) Turn left along West End and cycle out of the village. There is a parking area on the left along

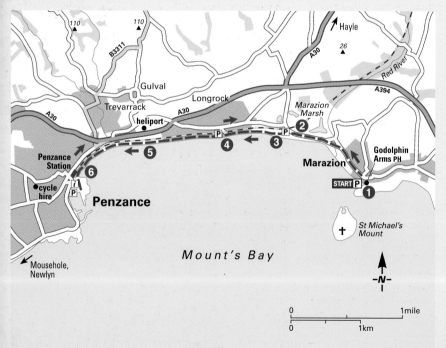

much of this road, so look out for people opening their car doors suddenly. Marazion Marsh lies to the right.

2 Where the road bears right to cross the main Penzance to Exeter railway line, keep straight ahead through a parking area, with the Pizza Shack (and toilets behind) on the right. Take care cycling through the car park.

3 Keep ahead and leave the car park to the left of the old station (now the Station pub), to join a level track that runs along the back of the beach. Follow this track, passing public toilets on the right.

4 Take care where the track drops downs to meet an entrance road to a beachside car park (there are warning notices 'Give way to traffic'). Pass through the parking area and continue along the track, with the railway close by on the right.

5 Go past the heliport, from which helicopters fly regularly to the Isles of Scilly, which lie more than 17 miles (28 km) southwest of Land's End (day trips are available). Pleasant views open up ahead towards Penzance.

6 On approaching the station the track narrows into a concrete walkway and becomes busier, so look out for pedestrians. Follow the track into the car park by Penzance railway and bus station, with the Tourist Information Centre to the right. There's lots to see in Penzance, which developed as an important pilchard fishing centre in medieval times. The coming of the Great Western Railway in Victorian times gave the town another boost and it is now the main centre in Penwith (the far western part of Cornwall). The harbour is full of interest, and it is from here that the RMV *Scillonian* makes regular sailings to the Isles of Scilly. When you've had your fill, relocate the Tourist Information Office, where you should turn round and return to Marazion. The First and Last Trail actually runs along the road to Newlyn and beyond, but the extended route is pretty busy in terms of traffic and therefore is not recommended for families with young children.

Route facts

DISTANCE/TIME. 5 miles (8km) 1h30

MAP OS Explorer 102 Land's End

START The Godolphin Arms car park, Marazion; grid ref: SW 516306

TRACKS Short stretch of road, track generally level, rough and bumpy in places

GETTING TO THE START From Penzance, take the A30 past the heliport. At the second roundabout turn right, signed Marazion. The Godolphin Arms car park is signed right (towards the beach).

THE PUB The Godolphin Arms, Marazion. Tel: 01736 710202; www. godolphinarms.co.uk

❶ Short stretch of road at the start and finish, one car park can be negotiated.

A Coastal Walk near St Ives

This walk starts from the maritime heart of St Ives and heads west along the glorious coastline. This is a very remote and wild part of the West Cornwall coast, a landscape of exquisite colours in spring and summer. Ancient field paths lead unswervingly back towards St Ives with a sequence of granite stiles recalling a very different world when folk travelled by foot out of necessity.

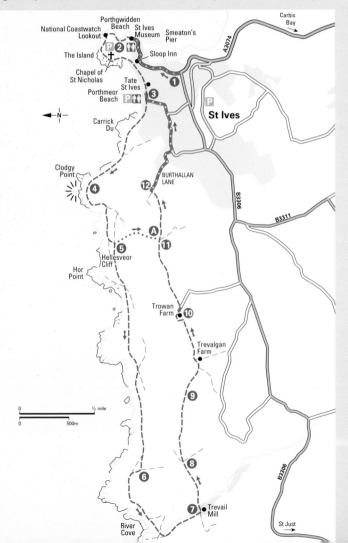

Route Directions

1 Walk along the harbour front towards Smeaton's Pier. Just before the pier entrance, turn left, signed 'St Ives Museum'. Where the road bends, keep straight on into Wheal Dream. Turn right past St Ives Museum, then follow a walkway to reach Porthgwidden Beach.

2 Cross the car park above the beach and climb to the National Coastwatch lookout. Go down steps, behind the building at the back of the lookout, then follow a footway to Porthmeor Beach. Go along the beach. At the beach end, go up to the car park.

3 Go up steps beside the public toilets, then turn right along a surfaced track past bowling and putting greens. Continue to the rocky headlands of Carrick Du and Clodgy Point.

4 From Clodgy Point continue to walk uphill and follow the path round to the right. Continue along a boggy and very rocky path. In about 0.5 mile (800m) go left at a junction by a small acorn signpost and big yellow-lichened boulder.

5 At a T-junction with a track just past a National Trust sign, 'Hellesveor Cliff', turn right to follow the coast path.

6 Keep right at a junction just past an old mine stack and shed inland. Continue to River Cove. On the other side of the cove, climb to where the path levels off at a junction. Follow the inland path.

7 At a junction with a track, go left through a kissing gate, then follow signs past Trevail Mill. Go through a kissing gate and climb steadily.

8 Cross a track and follow the hedged-in path, signposted 'Bridleway'. In 40yds (36m) go left over a stile by a black and white pole. Follow field-edges ahead over intervening stiles.

9 Keep in the field with a granite upright. Cross a stile. Where the field hedge bends sharply right, head across the field towards two gates. Cross a stile, continue to a stile at Trevalgan Farm. Go between buildings and in 50yds (46m), turn left at a gate, bear right and cross a stile. Continue to Trowan Farm.

10 At Trowan Farm, pass a granite post; continue between houses, go through a wooden field gate. Follow field paths over several stiles.

11 Cross a lane, then a stile and follow the left-edges of small fields. Pass a field gap on the left and turn left just before another and a rusty gate. Cross two stiles and pass between high hedges to a surfaced lane.

12 Turn right (Burthallan Lane) to a T-junction with the main road. Turn left, follow the road to Porthmeor Beach and the car park.

Route facts

DISTANCE/TIME. 8 miles (12.9km) 4h

MAP OS Explorer 102 Land's End

START Island car park, St Ives or Porthmeor Beach; grid ref: SW 522408

TRACKS Coastal path, can be quite rocky. Field paths, many stiles

GETTING TO THE START
St Ives is on the A3074 between Penzance and Camborne. Follow signs through the town centre, or off the B3306 west of the town centre, to Tate St Ives, to the Island car park at Porthgwidden Beach.

THE PUB The Sloop Inn, St Ives. Tel: 01736 796584

❶ The coast path can be rocky and wet in places; busy town streets.

PENDEEN   MAP REF SW3834

Pendeen is made up of a straggling line of small communities that were linked to tin and copper mines on the north coast of the Land's End peninsula. The smaller villages of Carnyorth, Trewellard, Boscaswell and Bojewyan make up the roll call of this last of Cornwall's coastal mining communities. The area's appeal is based on the startling conjunction of a fractured mining landscape and the raw beauty of the Atlantic coast. Pendeen's Geevor Mine was the mainstay of the larger area but the mine closed in 1991 in the face of international market pressures, and in spite of a spirited campaign by local people to save the industry. Surface freehold of Geevor is owned by Cornwall County Council and the complex has been imaginatively developed as a heritage centre, with mine workings, a museum and a fascinating underground tour.

Just south of Geevor is the National Trust's Levant Mine and Beam Engine, reached from Trewellard. At Levant, the silken power of steam is harnessed to a restored working beam engine.

PENWITH MOORS
MAP REF SW4535

Penwith Moors run parallel to the north coast of the Land's End Peninsula through an undulating series of hills that are crowned with granite tors. The high ground begins at Rosewall Hill just west of St Ives and is continuous throughout the beautiful parishes of Zennor and Morvah. Smaller areas of moorland continue the westward-leading sequence to Chapel Carn Brea above the wide, flat coastal plateau of Land's End itself. The moorland is a splendid counterpoint to the peninsula's outstanding coastline and is easily accessible from a number of points. Penwith Moors are noted for their ecological value and for their unique concentration of neolithic, Bronze Age and Iron Age remains, which include burial chambers, settlements, stone circles and standing stones. Most of the northern moors are at the heart of the Environmentally Sensitive Area within which farmers are compensated for working in sympathy with the traditional structure of the ancient landscape.

■ **Activity**

PREHISTORIC PEDAL

A cycle ride to ancient monuments – 20 miles (32km), mostly moderate with some steep gradients.
From Penzance, take the A30 west to Drift; turn right and pass Drift Reservoir then keep ahead following signs for 'Brane' and 'Carn Euny'. Visit Carn Euny Iron Age village on foot, then retrace your route and follow signs to Sancreed. Turn left beyond Sancreed church; continue to St Just then follow the B3306 north to Pendeen.

Beyond Pendeen, go left, signed 'Pendeen Lighthouse'. After half a mile (800m) go right to Pendeen Manor Farm and, with permission, view the Iron Age underground chamber. Return to the B3306 and continue left to Morvah. Turn right beyond Morvah, signed 'Madron' with a steep climb and descent to Bosullow. Opposite Men-an-Tol Studio, a track leads to Men-an-Tol, a probable remnant of a prehistoric burial chamber. From Bosullow follow the road to reach Lanyon Quoit. Return to Penzance through Madron.

PENZANCE MAP REF SW4730

Penzance has a sunny, friendly character gained from its south-facing position on the most sheltered part of Mount's Bay and from the bustle of its many attractive streets. It has the only promenade in Cornwall and it is a lengthy one, with wonderful views. The open-air, art deco Jubilee Swimming Pool rounds off the harbour end of the promenade. Penzance harbour is small but has a busy atmosphere and a mix of vessels from fishing boats to visiting yachts; the passenger boat to the Isles of Scilly leaves from the outer pier.

A pleasant approach to the harbour, from the busy Market Place, is down the diverting Chapel Street where there are antique and craft shops, pubs and eating houses. Penzance's attractive main street, Market Jew Street, is enhanced further by a raised granite terrace. There are shops of all kinds here, and in the pedestrianised Causewayhead that leads inland from Market Place. Towards the sea, and to either side of the Morrab Road, are Morrab Gardens and Penlee Park; the former is a lovely ornamental garden, the latter houses the Penlee House Gallery and Museum. The gallery stages excellent temporary exhibitions, often of work by the 19th- and early 20th-century Newlyn-based painters, such as Stanhope and Elizabeth Forbes, Walter Langley and 'Lamorna' Birch, who lived in the area from 1880 to 1940. The museum has good displays of local archaeology and the environment.

To the west, Penzance merges with Newlyn, the major fishing port in the southwest. Newlyn harbour is full of life

■ Visit

HIGH PLACES

Northeast of Sennen, the ground rises to Chapel Carn Brea, a smooth-browed hill (National Trust) and reached by turning off the A30 Land's End road at Crows-an-wra. There is a car park by the roadside from which a path leads to the summit. At various times in the past, Chapel Carn Brea was the site of a Bronze Age burial chamber, a medieval chapel and a beacon.

and colour. Scores of fishing boats of all types and sizes work from here in spite of the increasing difficulties of the modern international industry. The large fish market bustles with activity in the early morning as boats land a remarkable variety of fish. Parking at Newlyn is difficult, and most visitors find that a walk along Penzance's spacious promenade and on along the seafront to Newlyn is a pleasant alternative, which can be combined with a visit to the Newlyn Art Gallery along the way.

Just outside Penzance is the National Trust's Trengwainton Garden, a superb complex of five walled gardens set amid mature woodland, which is at its best during the spring and early summer months. Trengwainton Garden can be reached via Heamoor, or from Tremethick Cross on the St Just road.

Penzance has a summer festival called Golowan that lasts for eight days in late June and involves numerous cultural events and entertainment. It culminates in Mazey Day when the streets of Penzance are closed to traffic and the main street, Market Jew Street, hosts a street fair.

Prussia Cove Coastal Walk

A stroll through the coastal domain of one of Cornwall's most famous smugglers, John Carter. As you follow the walk inland, you will see the remote hamlets, lanes and paths, while the beach resounds with the sound of sea, where surfers and holiday-makers enjoy themselves.

Route Directions

1 From the Trenalls car park entrance walk back along the approach road, past the large house. Keep left and round the next sharp right-hand bend. Watch out for traffic. In about 150yds (138m), just past a field gate, walk through a hidden gap on the left, and into a field.

2 Follow the field-edge, bear off to the right, where it bends left, to reach a stile by a telegraph pole in the hedge opposite. Walk down the edge of the next field, behind Acton Castle (private). Turn right and follow the bottom field-edge to its end. Go over a stile and follow the next field-edge to cross an overgrown stile. Half-way along the next field, go left over a stile. Turn right along a lane.

3 Turn left along a track at a junction in front of a bungalow entrance at Trevean Farm. In 55yds (50m) by Trevean House keep right, up a stony track. Go through a gate on the right. Follow the left-hand edge of a long field to a stile on its top edge. Follow the right-hand edge of the next field.

4 At Trebarvah go over a stile and then through a gate. Cross a lane and continue across a stony area with houses on your right, (St Michael's Mount ahead), then follow a field-edge to a hedged-in path. Follow the path through fields, pass in front of some houses to reach the main road opposite the Victoria Inn. Go left and follow the road to the car park above Perranuthnoe Beach.

5 For the beach and café keep ahead. On the main route go left, just beyond the car park, and along a lane. Bear right at a fork, then bear right again just past a house at a junction. Go down a track towards the sea and follow it round left. Then, at a field entrance, go down right (signposted), turn sharp left through a gap and follow a broad track.

Route facts

DISTANCE/TIME 4 miles (6.4km) 3h

MAP OS Explorer 102 Land's End

START Trenalls, Prussia Cove. Small, privately owned car park; grid ref: SW 554282

TRACKS Good field paths and coastal paths, 18 stiles

GETTING TO THE START Prussia Cove is signposted off the A394 at Rosudgeon between Penzance and Helston, 6 miles (9.7km) east of Penzance. Follow the narrow lane to its end at Trenalls. The parking area is just past the farm at the end of the tarmac road, or park at Perranuthnoe, where the walk can be started at Point 5.

THE PUB The Victoria Inn, Perranuthnoe. Tel: 01736 710309; www.victoriainn-penzance.co.uk

❶ Care to be taken on the cliff path near Prussia Cove

6 At a junction above Trevean Cove, bear off right from the track and then join a path to walk along the cliff edge.

7 At the National Trust property of Cudden Point, follow the path steeply uphill and then across the inner slope of the headland above Piskies Cove.

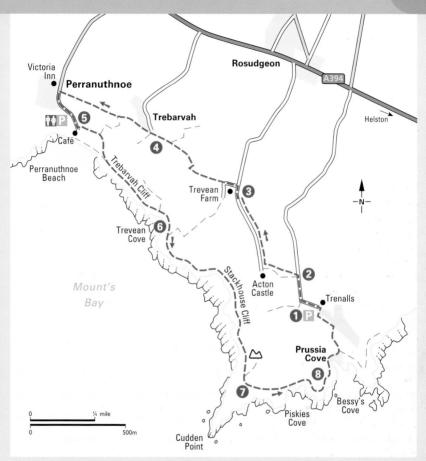

8 Go through a gate and pass some fishing huts. Continue round the edge of the Bessy's Cove inlet of Prussia Cove, and go up steps to a track by a thatched cottage. The cove can be reached down a path on the right just before this junction. Turn right and follow the track, past a post box. Keep left at junctions, to return to the car park.

What to look for

Along the paths and fields east of Perranuthnoe, the feathery leafed tamarisk (*Tamarix anglica*), lends an Mediterranean atmosphere to the Cornish scene. Tamarisk is often planted in coastal regions as a windbreak because of its resilience and its ability to survive the battering of salt-laden winds. Take time midway in the walk to enjoy Perranuthnoe Beach, known as Perran Sands, a fine south-facing beach, which catches the sun all day. It's also worth exploring Prussia Cove itself and its individual rocky inlets.

PORTHCURNO MAP REF SW3822

The pure, golden sand of Porthcurno's beaches and the crystal clear clarity of its sea supports Cornwall's claim to be an alternative to the Mediterranean. Under a blazing summer sun, the comparison is apt. Granite towers and pinnacles lie embedded in the steep vegetated slopes that encircle the bay and the superb sand lies deeply against the shoreline. Some of the adjoining beaches are covered at high tide but the main Porthcurno beach is always available, clean, sparkling and luxurious.

For many years Porthcurno was the centre of international cable telegraphy. From here, undersea telegraph cables communicated with the rest of the world and, at one time, the Cable and Wireless Company ran a training college in the Porthcurno Valley. In 1994, Porthcurno beach and its adjacent cliff land was given to the National Trust by the company, which had relocated its main training facilities to Coventry. There is a fascinating telegraph museum housed in underground chambers within the old Porthcurno college complex just inland from the large car park.

The visitor to Porthcurno is really spoiled for choice. The main beach is marvellously persuasive for wriggling the toes; but to either side lie lovely coastal walks. Eastward is the famous Logan Rock, a vast monolith that once rocked at the touch of a finger but is less responsive now, and westward are Minack Theatre, Porth Chapel beach and the little Church of St Levan. St Levan can also be reached along the narrow road that climbs steeply uphill from Porthcurno. There is a car park by the church. All around Porthcurno Bay you will find sheltered coves, such as Penberth, and exquisite tidal beaches, and the eastern side is flanked by the magnificent headland of Treryn Dinas.

PORTHGWARRA
MAP REF SW3721

Porthgwarra lies to the southwest of Porthcurno and is sheltered from the prevailing Atlantic winds by high ground that culminates at the magnificent granite cliff of Chair Ladder at Gwennap Head, the most southerly extent of the Land's End Peninsula. At Porthgwarra, tunnels have been carved through the softer rock of flanking promontories to allow access to the beach by donkey and trap in the days when neighbouring farmers collected seaweed to fertilise their fields. The cliff-top walks to the west are magnificent and the area is noted for rare species of birds that often make landfall here during spring and autumn migrations.

ST IVES MAP REF SW5140

St Ives' rare character springs from its fishing traditions, its artistic inheritance, and its tourism industry. There is a clash of style amongst all three at times, but St Ives has survived such competing interests. Not only is the town the archetypal Cornish fishing port, it also has magnificent beaches of silken sand that offer both safe family bathing and surf to sing about. The town has aimed determinedly upmarket in recent years and has benefited greatly from the opening of the Tate St Ives in 1993.

■ Visit

TRENCROM HILL

The fine rocky hill of Trencrom, the site of an Iron Age encampment, stands above the Hayle Estuary and can be reached from Lelant or from the B3311 St Ives to Penzance road. Trencrom is in the care of the National Trust and there is a small car park on its southern side. The path to the summit is short and steep in places, but the views are outstanding. Just west of Trencrom is the little village of Nancledra from where the green and peaceful Towednack Valley runs north to the sea through a gap in the coastal hills.

The gallery stands above Porthmeor Beach, its curves and crests are as white as the waves below. The paintings on display are by leading artists of the St Ives School including Patrick Heron, Peter Lanyon and Terry Frost. It is a joy to find such paintings within the very landscape that inspired them. The view seaward from the gallery's roof terrace is worth crossing the world for. Before the Tate opened, the Barbara Hepworth Museum and Sculpture Garden was the most important artistic attraction here and still remains popular.

But St Ives is a delight overall because of its narrow, canyon-like streets, ubiquitous granite cobbles, and clear, sea-mirrored light. The parish church of St Ia is one of the finest in Cornwall. St Ives harbour area, known locally as 'Downlong', is a maze of exquisite vernacular granite buildings where you catch satisfying glimpses of shady courtyards and passageways. And there are always those beaches to escape to: Porthminster to the south is sheltered and calm; Porthmeor to the north is a bit more lively and popular with the surfing crowd.

There are several smaller beaches at the harbour and in the lee of the Island, the breezy, green promontory that juts out to sea from a low-lying neck of land. The price of all this is potential overcrowding at the busiest holiday periods. Avoid dawdling through St Ives by car and be prepared for close-quarters humanity in the narrow Fore Street and along the busy harbour front. There is a park-and-ride scheme at Trenwith above the town and another at Lelant Station, southeast of the town, which uses a little branch line. Artistic ambience – and, at times, pretension – means that St Ives has numerous galleries and craft shops. There is an excellent town museum at Wheal Dream, and most of the town's numerous restaurants and pubs are of quality and character.

ST JUST   MAP REF SW3731

There is a generous market square at the heart of this sturdy Cornish town. At the eastern corner of the crowded square stands the parish church, a lovely 15th-century building in good weathered granite, with a square tower and a handsome interior. Market Square has a number of friendly pubs and there are cafés and a good selection of shops in which to browse within the square and in the streets that radiate from it. St Just is the ideal base from which to explore the famous mining coast of the Land's End Peninsula.

The elegant headland of Cape Cornwall lies to the west; it is rugged, yet shapely and its rounded summit is crowned with the chimney stack of a long defunct mine. On the southern edge of the cape is Priest's Cove from where small fishing boats work. From the cove, a stony track leads up to the rocky headland of Carn Gloose from where the impressive burial chamber of Ballowall lies about 150 yards (137m) inland. The cape, and coastline to either side, is in the care of the National Trust.

To the north lies the remarkable mining area of Kenidjack and the Nancherrow Valley, a historic mining landscape that is being preserved by the Trust. A mile (1.2km) north of the town along the B3306 is the village of Botallack and the nearby coastal area is particularly rich in old mine buildings.

SENNEN MAP REF SW3525

The Atlantic truly begins at Sennen's Whitesand Bay where the west-facing beaches can be exhilarating when the surf is high. Gwenver Beach to the north is a 'serious' surfing and body-boarding beach that is also delightful for soaking up the sun, though close attention should be paid to safety flags and to lifeguards. Tidal currents can be fierce. Sennen Beach is the larger of the two. It is less adventurous but just as delightful and is easily accessible from the car park at Sennen Cove.

Sennen is in two halves. The village proper is on the higher ground alongside the A30. Sennen Cove has the main attractions of the beaches and fine granite cliffs to the south. A car park at the far end gives access to the cliff path and to Land's End on foot. This southern end of the cove spills into the ocean and has a brisk sea-going atmosphere with a narrow quay edging into the sea – to be avoided during rough conditions – and a lifeboat house with a modern lifeboat. The nearby wood and granite Round House contained the capstan that was used for hauling boats out of the water. It is now a craft shop and gallery.

ZENNOR MAP REF SW4538

Storm-tumbled cliffs and wheeling gulls, guard Penwith's wild, Atlantic shoreline. The sleepy village of Zennor with its rough tawny hills slope down towards the echoing sea cliffs. Between hills and sea lies a narrow coastal plateau of small irregular fields whose Cornish 'hedges' of rough granite date from the Iron Age. Because of its antiquity this long-farmed landscape has earned Zennor protected status for ecological and archaeological reasons. Such vulnerability should be taken into account when visiting Zennor and its surrounding countryside. Below the car park is the Wayside Museum; it is

■ Visit

A SCENIC ROUTE
One of the finest scenic drives in England is to the north of Sennen along the B3306 coast road. The section between Morvah and St Ives is quite spectacular. The road winds its sinuous way between mottled moorland and the patchworked web of Iron Age fields that cluster together along the narrow coastal plateau above a glittering sea. There are pubs along the way and several cream-tea havens.

crammed with exhibits about farming, mining, archaeology and folklore. Zennor's Church of St Senara lords it rather handsomely over the village.

Zennor has an endearing myth of a mermaid. The mermaid was said to have seduced a local chorister into the dark waters below the lofty Zennor Head. On quiet evenings, the smooth heads of seals perpetuate the legend and an attractive bench-end motif in the church encourages the tale.

Access to Zennor Head and to the coast path is on foot down a narrow lane that starts behind the Tinner's Arms. Zennor Head has a flat top, but its western flank is spectacular. Towering cliffs fall darkly into a narrow gulf, the sea crashes white against the shoreline far below. If you can tear yourself away from thoughts of mermaids, it is an invigorating 6-mile (9.6km) walk eastwards to St Ives along some of the most remote coastline in Cornwall.

■ Visit

GURNARD'S HEAD

Just over a mile (1.2km) to the west of Zennor Head lies Gurnard's Head, a long, elegant promontory that rises to a great gnarled headland ringed with sheer black cliffs. There are remains of embankments across the neck of this Iron Age site and on the flanking slopes are the rough remains of Iron Age houses. Gurnard's Head may be reached from the B3306, at the Gurnard's Head Hotel, a mile (1.6km) southwest of Zennor, but parking is limited. The coast path between Zennor Head and Gurnard's Head makes for a pleasantly rough walk of about 1.5 miles (2.4km). Both headlands are in the care of the National Trust.

THE ISLES OF SCILLY

MAP REF SV9111

The Isles of Scilly are famously known as the 'Fortunate Islands' or the 'Sunshine Islands'. They deserve the superlatives, though their beauty and uniqueness require no exaggeration.

The hundred or so islands and islets that make up the archipelago lie just 28 miles (45km) west-southwest of Land's End as the crow flies. Only five islands are inhabited – St Agnes, Bryher, St Mary's, St Martin's, and Tresco – and together they offer a rare combination of seascapes, golden beaches and crystal-clear sea, with quiet green corners inland.

Bryher Bryher lies amidst the northwestern group of islands that include Tresco. It is 1.5 miles (2.4km) long and barely half a mile (0.8km) across at its widest point. Bryher faces Tresco across the narrow channel of New Grimsby Sound and island life is focused on the beaches that fringe the Sound. Here boats draw up at a granite quay, or at the jetty, built as one of Aneka Rice's famous television 'challenges' to extend landing times on Bryher and now known as 'Annequay'.

St Agnes Just over 1 mile (1.6km) wide, This island has a special atmosphere of serenity. It is the most southerly of the group and is separated from St Mary's by the deep water channel of St Mary's Sound. The Turk's Head Inn and the Post Office are at the hub of the community. To the east the main island is linked by a narrow sandbar to the smaller tidal 'island' of Gugh and off its western shore is the protected bird island of Annet.

Beyond Annet lie the dramatic Western Rocks – reefs that end at the Bishop Rock Lighthouse.

St Martin's The most northerly island in the group, St Martin's is 2 miles (3.2km) in length and just over half a mile (800m) wide. Landing on St Martin's can be adventurous at certain states of the tide, when walking the plank to reach the sandy shore from launches is necessary. Walking here is exhilarating, though the lure of magnificent beaches such as Great Bay on St Martin's northern shore tends to distract.

St Mary's St Mary's is the largest of the Isles of Scilly. Its main settlement of Hugh Town is the marine metropolis of the islands, and it is from Hugh Town Quay that the passenger launches leave for the exciting sea-trips that are an essential part of holidaying on Scilly. There are beaches on the north and south side of Hugh Town, the southern bay of Porth Cressa being particularly delightful. A footpath follows the coastline for a 9-mile (14.4km) circuit, passing several well-preserved prehistoric sites on the way. Early flower growing developed in Scilly from the late 1860s. Daffodils and narcissi are still exported from the islands, but the trade has declined in recent years.

Tresco Tresco lies at the sheltered heart of the islands. It is more of a show-place than the rest of Scilly, a private domain where there is an atmosphere of carefully regulated life and of gentle pace. The exquisite subtropical gardens surrounding Tresco Abbey House are the main focus of the island. A priory to St Nicholas was

■ Activity

BEST BOAT TRIPS IN BRITAIN?
Scillonians are outstanding seamen, and the tradition of small-boat handling is maintained by the fishermen and by the boatmen who run pleasure trips. These boat trips are an essential part of getting the best from a visit to the Scilly Isles. The inter-island launches connect daily to St Mary's and also make trips between the islands. Some of the finest trips are those to the outlying uninhabited islands and to the marine wildernesses of the Western Rocks, the Norrard Rocks and the Eastern Isles, where puffins and seabirds can be seen at close quarters and where seals lie at their ease on sea-sucked ledges.

■ Activity

LIVE AND LIVELY ENTERTAINMENT
Entertainment on the Isles of Scilly is of a richly traditional nature. There are numerous slide shows and delightful talks in the local community hall of each of the islands. Island boatmen especially are noted for their salty wit. Cricket is popular, and visitors are often press-ganged into making up teams. Watch out, extremely competent islanders are often matched against mainland elevens. Don't even think of mentioning mid-on or mid-off.

established by Benedictine monks during the 12th century; the scant ruins that remain are now incorporated into the Abbey Gardens, where Burmese Honeysuckle, Australian Scarlet Bottle-brush, Aloes, Dracaenas, Mimosa, gigantic ice plants, and a host of other exotics line the terraced pathways. Tresco has a heliport from where connections can be made to Penzance. Dogs must be kept on leads on Tresco.

TOURIST INFORMATION CENTRES

St Ives
The Guildhall, Street-an-Pol.
Tel: 01736 796297;
www.stives-cornwall.co.uk

Penzance
Station Approach.
Tel: 01736 362207;
www.visit-westcornwall.co.uk

Hayle
Hayle Library, Commercial
Road (seasonal opening).
Tel: 01736 754399

St Just
Library, Market Street.
Tel: 01736 788165

Isles of Scilly
Hugh Town, St Mary's.
Tel: 01720 424031;
www.simplyscilly.co.uk

PLACES OF INTEREST

Barbara Hepworth Museum and Sculpture Garden
Barnoon Hill, St Ives.
Tel: 01736 796226;
www.tate.org.uk/stives

Chysauster Ancient Village
Newmill. Tel: 07831 757934;
www.english-heritage.org.uk

Geevor Tin Mine
Pendeen. Tel: 01736 788662;
www.geevor.com

Levant Mine and Beam Engine
Trewellard.
Tel: 01736 786156

Marazion Town Museum
Town Hall, The Square.
Tel: 01736 711061

Minack Theatre
Porthcurno.
Tel: 01736 810181;
www.minack.com

Mousehole Wild Bird Hospital and Sanctuary
Raginnis Hill.
Tel: 01736 731386

Newlyn Art Gallery
New Road, Newlyn,
Penzance. Tel: 01736 363715;
www.newlynartgallery.co.uk

Penlee House Gallery and Museum
Penlee Park, Morrab Road.
Tel: 01736 363625;
www.penleehouse.org.uk

Penwith Gallery
Back Road West, St Ives.
Tel: 01736 795579

Porthcurno Telegraph Museum
Porthcurno.
Tel: 01736 810966;
www.porthcurno.org.uk

St Ives Museum
Wheal Dream.
Tel: 01736 796005

St Mary's, Scilly Isles, Isles of Scilly Museum
Church Street, Hugh Town.
Tel: 01720 422337;
www.iosmuseum.org

St Michael's Mount
Marazion.
Tel: 01736 710507;
www.stmichaelsmount.co.uk

Tate St Ives
Porthmeor Beach, St Ives.
Tel: 01736 796226;
www.tate.org.uk

Trengwainton Garden
Madron, Penzance.
Tel: 01736 363148

Trereife
Trereife, Penzance.
Tel: 01736 362750;
www.trereifepark.co.uk

Tresco, Isles of Scilly, Abbey Garden and Valhalla Museum
Tel: 01720 424108;
www.tresco.co.uk

Trewidden Garden
Buryas Bridge, Penzance.
Tel: 01736 363021;
www.trewiddengarden.co.uk

FOR CHILDREN

Paradise Park
Trelissick Road, Hayle.
Tel: 01736 751020; www.
paradisepark.org.uk

SHOPPING

Penzance
Chapel Street has antiques
and crafts shops.

St Ives
Art galleries and crafts shops
in the Fore Street area.

LOCAL SPECIALITIES

CRAFTS
Gem and Jewellery
Workshop, Pendeen.
Tel: 01736 788217.
Chapel Street, Penzance.
The Round House,
Sennen. Tel: 01736 871859;
www.round-house.co.uk

◼ PERFORMING ARTS

Acorn Arts Centre
Parade Street, Penzance.
Tel: 01736 365520;
www.acornartscentre.co.uk
Minack Theatre
Porthcurno. Open-air
performances, summer only.
Tel: 01736 810181;
www.minack.com

◼ SPORTS & ACTIVITIES

ANGLING
Sea
St Ives, Penzance,
Mousehole.
Coarse
South West Lakes Trust.
Tel: 01566 771930;
www.swlakestrust.org.uk
BEACHES
*Lifeguards, where indicated,
are on summer service. Dogs
are not allowed on several
popular beaches from Easter
Day to 1st October. During
winter, when dogs are allowed,
owners must use poop scoops.*
Carbis Bay
Safe bathing. Lifeguard.
Hayle
Hayle Towans; Mexico
Towans, Upton Towans
and Gwithian: Generally
safe bathing. Surfing.
Lifeguards.
Marazion
Windsurfing. Lifeguard.
Penzance
Long Rock Beach: shingle
and sand, safe bathing.

Perranuthnoe
Safe bathing, but sandbank
may form at centre of beach.
Porthcurno
Safe bathing, but take care
during high tide. Lifeguard.
Sennen
Gwynver: Bathing between
flags only;
Sennen: Blue Flag Award,
Seaside Award. Surfing,
bathing between flags only.
Lifeguard.
St Ives
Porthminster: safe bathing.
Lifeguard.
Porthmeor: Blue Flag Award,
Seaside Award, surfing
beach, generally safe bathing.
Lifeguard.
BOAT TRIPS
Penzance
Isles of Scilly Steamship
Company. Day trips to Isles of
Scilly. Tel: 0845 710 5555;
www.ios-travel.co.uk
Marine Discovery
Excursions to see seals,
seabirds, sharks and
dolphins. Tel: 01736 874907;
www.marinediscovery.co.uk
St Ives
Sea cruises from the harbour.
CYCLE HIRE
Hayle
Hayle Cycles, 36 Penpol
Terrace. Tel: 01736 753825;
www.haylecycles.com
Penzance
The Cycle Centre, New Street.
Tel: 01736 351671

Pedals Bike Hire, Kiosk 17,
Wharfside Shopping Centre.
Tel: 01730 360600
HORSE-RIDING
Lelant Downs
Old Mill Stables.
Tel: 01736 753045
Penzance
Mulfra Trekking Centre,
Newmill. Tel: 01736 361601
WATERSPORTS
Hayle
Shore Surf School.
Tel: 01736 755556;
www.shoresurf.com
St Ives
WindandSea, 25 Fore Street.
Tel: 01736 794830

◼ CUSTOMS & EVENTS

Hayle
Hayle Heritage Week, Aug.
Mousehole
Sea, Salts and Sail Festival,
Jul.
Newlyn
Newlyn Fish Festival,
Aug Bank Holiday Mon.
Penzance
Golowan Festival and Mazey
Day, Jun.
www.golowan.co.uk
St Ives
St Ives Feast Day, early Feb.
St Ives Festival of Music and
the Arts, early Sep.
St Just
Lafrowda Festival, Jul.
The Isles of Scilly
World Pilot Gig Racing
Championships Apr–May.

Tea Rooms

Orangery Café

**Penlee House Gallery &
Museum, Morrab Road
Penzance TR18 4HE
Tel: 01736 363625;
www.penleehouse.org.uk**
Follow an enlightening
gallery tour with lunch or
afternoon tea in the café.
Cakes and pastries are
freshly baked, lunches
include crab sandwiches,
quiche, and fish pie.

Godrevy Café

**Godrevy Towans, Gwithian,
Hayle TR27 5ED
Tel: 01736 757999**
Godrevy Café stands isolated
within the dunes at Godrevy
Beach. Beautifully designed,
it has spacious terraces
which make the most of the
view, and an unusual attic
dining space. It's open all day,
for breakfast, coffee and
cakes, a light lunch, or watch
the sunset as you dine from
the evening restaurant menu.

Porthgwidden Café

**Porthgwidden Beach ,
St Ives TR26 1PL
Tel: 01736 796791;
www.porthgwiddencafe.
co.uk**
A relaxed and intimate café
with a notably Moroccan feel
on the quietest beach in
St Ives. Call in for smoked

salmon and scrambled egg,
freshly baked muffins or
croissants from 8am. Pick a
sunny day and head straight
for the terrace for cracking
views. Lunches take in
mussels with coconut and
basil broth, and fresh crayfish
baguettes. Afternoon teas on
the terrace are an experience
to savour as are the
Mediterranean-style dinners
in the evening.

Pubs

Star Inn

**Fore Street, St Just TR19 7LL
Tel: 01736 788767;
www.thestarinn-stjust.co.uk**
St Just's oldest pub has a
low-beamed bar, a polished
slate floor, glowing coal fires
and walls packed with mining
and seafaring memorabilia.
Pop in to experience the
homely, unspoilt atmosphere
and the St Austell beer.

Tinners Arms

**Zennor, St Ives TR26 3BY
Tel: 01736 796927;
www.tinnersarms.com**
A former tin miners' local, it
is now an oasis for walkers
tackling the St Ives to Zennor
coastal walk. Two open fires
warm the bar, filled with
flagstones, and pine tables,
where you can rest and refuel
on Sharp's ales, fresh fish
and locally reared meats.

The Gurnard's Head

**Treen, Zennor TR26 3DE
Tel: 01736 796928;
www.gurnardshead.co.uk**
The menu changes daily and
includes fresh Newlyn fish
and local farm meats. Crab
and fish stew, herb-crusted
John Dory and rib-eye steak
with red onion marmalade
will not disappoint, nor will
the Skinner's ales.

Old Coastguard Inn

**The Parade, Mousehole
TR19 6PR. Tel: 01736 731222;
www.oldcoastguardhotel.
co.uk**
This one-time coastguard
station is perched high above
the village. Although more of
a hotel than pub, there is a
light and airy bar with real ale
on tap. Contemporary menus
take in delicious lunchtime
soups, sandwiches and
salads, and fresh fish.

Navy Inn

**Lower Queen Street,
Penzance TR18 4DE
Tel: 01736 333232;
www.navyinn.co.uk**
A contemporary gastro-pub
that is popular with locals.
Expect up-to-the-minute
culinary ideas and quality
local produce, notably fresh
fish and seafood in the form
of hake poached in saffron
sauce, and Newlyn crab.

■ OTHER INFORMATION

Coastguard

Dial 999 and ask for the Coastguard Service, which co-ordinates rescue services.

Cornwall Wildlife Trust

Five Acres, Allet, Truro.

Tel: 01872 273939; www.cornwallwildlifetrust.org.uk

English Heritage

South West Regional Office, 29 Queen Square, Bristol.

Tel: 0117 975 0700

www.english-heritage.org.uk

National Trust in Cornwall

Lanhydrock, Bodmin.

Tel: 01208265200;

www.nationaltrust.org.uk

Health

Information on health problems is available from NHS Direct.

Tel: 0845 4647;

www.nhsdirect.nhs.uk

Dental Helpline

Tel: 0845 063 1188

Environment Agency

Manley House, Kestrel Way, Exeter.

Tel: 08708 506 506;

www.environment-agency.gov.uk

Angling

Numerous opportunities for fishing on farms, lakes and rivers. Permits and licences are available from local tackle shops and TICs.

Public Transport

Timetable for bus, coach, rail, ferry and air services in Cornwall is available from Passenger Transport Unit, County Hall, Truro.

Tel: 0300 1234 222; www.cornwallpublictransport.info

Parking

Information on parking permits and car parks in the area is available from local TICs.

Places of Interest

There will be an admission charge unless otherwise stated. We give details of just some of the facilities within the area covered by this guide. Further information can be obtained from local TICs or the web.

Weather Call

Southwest weather details.

Tel: 09068 500 404

Beaches

Lifeguards, where indicated, are on summer service. Dogs are not allowed on several popular beaches from Easter to 1st October. During winter, when dogs are allowed, owners are asked to use poop scoops. For more information on beaches in Cornwall visit www.cornwall-beaches.co.uk; www.cornwallbeachguide.co.uk

Surf Call

Tel: 09068 360 360

Cycling

A network of quiet lanes offers good cycling between the main roads and centres of the area. Please note that cycling is not allowed on public footpaths or on the coast path. Some woodland areas have excellent cycle routes; leaflets are available from local TICs.

■ ORDNANCE SURVEY MAPS

SOUTHEAST CORNWALL

Explorer 1:25,000;

Sheets 107, 108, 109

Landranger 1:50,000;

Sheets 200, 201

NORTH CORNWALL

Explorer 1:25,000;

Sheets 106, 109, 111, 112

Landranger 1:50,000;

Sheets 190, 200

MID-CORNWALL

Explorer 1:25,000;

Sheets 104, 105, 106

Landranger 1:50,000;

Sheets 200, 203, 204

LIZARD PENINSULA

Explorer 1:25,000;

Sheets 102, 103, 104

Landranger 1:50,000;

Sheets 203, 204

LAND'S END PENINSULA

Explorer 1:25,000;

Sheet 102

Landranger 1:50,000;

Sheet 203

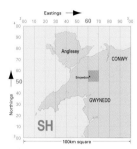

Eastings ➡

SH

100km square

Eastings ➡

10km

The National Grid system covers Great Britain with an imaginary network of grid squares. Each is 100km square in area and is given a unique alphabetic reference, as shown in the diagram above.

These squares are sub-divided into one hundred 10km squares, identified by vertical lines (eastings) and horizontal lines (northings). The reference for the square a feature is located within is made by adding the numbers of the two lines which cross in the bottom left corner of that square to the alphabetic reference (ignoring the small figures). The easting is quoted first. For example, SH6050.

For a 2-figure reference, the zeros are omitted, giving just SH65. In this book, we use 4-figure references, which allow us to pinpoint the feature more accurately by dividing the 10km square into one hundred 1km squares. These squares are not actually printed on the road atlas but are estimated by eye. The same process is carried out as before, giving an enhanced reference of SH6154.

Key to Atlas

M4	Motorway with number	Toll	Toll	⛪	Abbey, cathedral or priory	NTS	National Trust for Scotland property
S Fleet	Motorway service area		Road under construction	🐟	Aquarium	🐦	Nature reserve
	Motorway toll		Narrow Primary route with passing places	♜	Castle	★	Other place of interest
11	Motorway junction with and without number	→	Steep gradient	⌒	Cave		
3	Restricted motorway junctions			♛	Country park	P+R	Park and Ride location
	Motorway and junction under construction	—○—✕—	Railway station and level crossing	🏏	County cricket ground	♣	Picnic site
A3	Primary route single/dual carriageway	+++++++	Tourist railway	🐄	Farm or animal centre	🚂	Steam centre
BATH	Primary route destinations	– – – –	National trail	❀	Garden	🎿	Ski slope natural
	Roundabout	············	Forest drive	⚑	Golf course	🎿	Ski slope artificial
5	Distance in miles between symbols	⌣⌣⌣	Heritage coast	🏛	Historic house	i	Tourist Information Centre
A1123	Other A Road single/dual carriageway	⛴	Ferry route	🐎	Horse racing	☼	Viewpoint
B2070	B road single/dual carriageway	6	Walk start point	🏁	Motor racing	V	Visitor or heritage centre
	Unclassified road single/dual carriageway	1	Cycle start point	🏛	Museum	🐾	Zoological or wildlife collection
		✈	Airport				
⊢=====⊣	Road tunnel	3	Tour start point	Ⓗ	Heliport		Forest Park
				✗	Windmill		National Park (England & Wales)
				NT	National Trust property		National Scenic Area (Scotland)

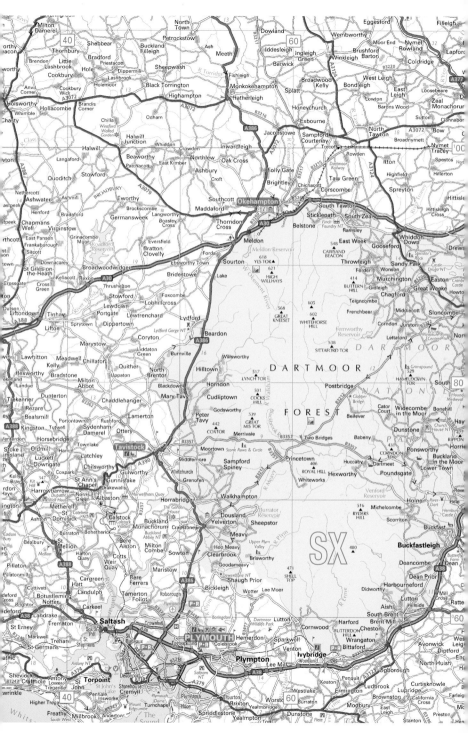

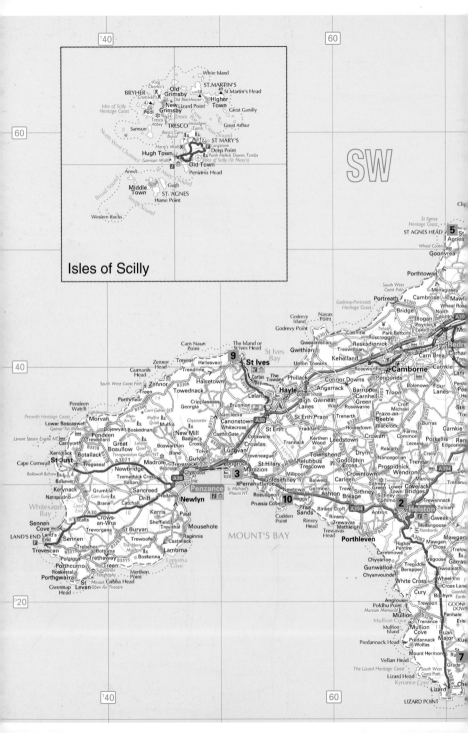

Isles of Scilly

White Island

ST.MARTIN'S

St Martin's Head

King Charles's

Old Grimsby

Old Blockhouse

Old Lizard Point

Higher Town

Great Ganilly

BRYHER

Cromwell's

New Grimsby

Tresco

Tresco Abbey

Innisidgen Tomb

Great Arthur

Pool

TRESCO

Isles of Scilly Heritage Coast

North West Channel

Samson

Bant's Carn Burial

Crow Sound

ST MARY'S

Harry's Walls

Hugh Town

Longstone

Deep Point

Garrison Walk

Porth Hellick Downs Tombs

Isles of Scilly (St Mary's)

Old Town

Peninnis Head

St Mary's Sound

Annet

Gugh

Broad Sound

Middle Town

Horse Point

ST. AGNES

St Agnes Heritage Coast

ST AGNES HEAD

5 St Agnes

Wheal Coates

Smith Sound

Western Rocks

Goonvrea

Porthtowan

Menagissey

Mawl

South West Coast Path

Portreath

Cambrose

B3300

Wheal Rose

Godrevy-Portreath Heritage Coast

Bridge

Illogan

North Country

A30

Mo

Godrevy Island

Navax Point

B3301

Poynter's Lane End

Park Bottom

Roscroggan

Redr

Godrevy Point

Coombe

Gwealavellan

Reskadinnick

Carn Brea

Carhar

Gwithian

Treswithian

Camborne

Carnkie

Lanr

Carn Naun Point

The Island or St Ives Head

St Ives Bay

Upton Towans

Roseworthy

Connor Downs

Penh

Four Lanes

Zennor Head

Treveal

Hellesveor

Phillack

9 St Ives

Angarrack

Barripper

Troon

Bolenow

Gurnards Head

Trendrine

Carbis Bay

The Towans

Carnhell Green

Croft Michael

Praze-an-Beeble

Burras

Halsetown

Lelant

Hayle

High Gwinear

Rosewarne

Carnkie

South West Coast Path

B3306

Towednack

Brunnion

Lanes

Ran

Treen

Zennor

Cripplesease

Nancledra

Fraddam

Horsedown

Crowan

Porkellis

Edgcombe

Penwith Heritage Coast

Pendeen Watch

Morvah

Porthmeor

Georgia

St Erth Praze

Trenerth

Common

Lezerea

Men-An-Tol

Carn Galver

Whitecross

Leedstown

Releath

Trennear

Treng

A394

Lighthouse

Mulfra Quoit

Mulfra

New Mill

Castle Gate

St Erth

Trannack

Kerthen Wood

Townshend

Drym

Nancegollan

Trebarv

Geevor Tin Mines

Bojewyan

Boskednan

Boswarthan

Badger's Cross

Trevenenague

Godolphin Cross

Prospidnick

Manhay

Levant Steam Engine NT

Pendeen Trewellard

Great Bosullow

Lanyon Quoit

Bone

Gulval

Crowlas

Relubbus

Crownton

Wendron

Carnyorth

Trengwainton Gardens NT

Madron

Ludgvan

St Hilary

Balwest

Sithney Green

Lower Town

Coverack Bridges

Botallack

B3318

Heamoor

Trevarrack

Longrock

Marazion

Trescowe

Millpool

Carleen

Breage

Sithney Common

Cape Cornwall

St Just

Tregeseal

Newbridge

Tremethick Cross

Chyandour

A30

St Michael's Mount NT

Goldsithney

Perranuthnoe

Newtown

Germoe

Trew

Ashton

2 Helston

Ballowall Barrow

Kelynack

Grumbla

Sancreed

Sellan

Penzance

Rosudgeon

neggy

Trewennack

Nanquidno

Brane

Catchall

Drift

Newlyn

Prussia Cove

Praa Sands

Rinsey Croft

A394

Antron

Gweek

Whitesand Bay

Land's End

Crows-an-Wra

Tredavoe

Kerris

Cudden Point

Rinsey

Trewavas

Rinsey Head

Mellangoose

Flambards

Tolvan

Escalls

A30

Sheffield

Trevithal

Paul

Mousehole

Trewavas Head

Methleigh

10

Green

Tolvan

Sennen Cove

Trevorgans

St Buryan

Raginnis

MOUNT'S BAY

Porthleven

Higher Pentire

Mawgan

LAND'S END

Land's End

Sennen

Trebehor

Treen

The Merry Maidens

Castallack

Lamorna

Carminowe

Tregoose

Trelo

Trevescan

Bottoms

Boskenna

Garras

Polgigga

Tretheway

B3315

Lamorna Cove

Chyvarloe

Gunwalloe

Tregidden Bereppe

Gwealeath

Porthcurno

Roskestal

Treen

Submarine Telegraphy

Merthen Point

White Cross

Wheel Inn

Cross Lanes

Porthgwarra

Gwennap Head

Minack Open Air Theatre

Levan

Gribba Head

Cury

Trewoon

Bochym

GOONH

DOW

Angrouse

Poldhu Point

Mullion

Penhale

Marconi Memorial

Trenance

Eris

Mullion Cove

Mullion Island

Mullion Cove

Ruan Major

St

Predannack Head

Predannack Wollas

Mount Hermon

7

The Lizard Heritage Coast

Vellan Head

Ru

Che

Lizard Head

South West Coast Path

Grade

Kynance Cove

Lizard

LIZARD POINT

SW

The Automobile Association would like to thank the following photographers and companies for their assistance in the preparation of this book. Abbreviations for the picture credits are as follows – (t) top; (b) bottom; (c) centre; (l) left; (r) right; (AA) AA World Travel Library

1 AA/John Wood; 4/5 AA/John Wood; 8tl AA/Roger Moss; 8tr AA/Caroline Jones; 8cl AA/Neil Ray; 8cr AA/John Wood; 8b AA/John Wood; 9 AA/John Wood; 10t AA/Andrew Lawson; 10b AA/Andrew Lawson; 11t AA/John Wood; 11bl AA/John Wood; 11br AA/Roger Moss; 13 AA/Caroline Jones; 14 AA/Caroline Jones; 18/19 AA/Neil Ray; 21tl AA/Caroline Jones; 21tr AA/Rupert Tenison; 21b AA/Roger Moss; 22c AA/John Wood; 22b AA/Rupert Tenison; 23t AA/John Wood; 23c AA/Roger Moss; 23b AA/Roger Moss; 32 AA/Caroline Jones; 38 AA/John Wood; 40/41 AA/John Wood; 43tl AA/Roger Moss; 43tr AA/John Wood; 43b AA/John Wood; 44cl AA/Rupert Tenison; 44cr AA/John Wood; 44b AA/John Wood; 45t AA/Roger Moss; 45c AA/Roger Moss; 45b AA/John Wood; 49 AA/John Wood; 55 AA/John Wood; 61 AA/John Wood; 65 AA/John Wood; 68 AA/John Wood; 70/71 AA/John Wood; 73tl AA/Roger Moss; 73tr AA/Roger Moss; 73b AA/John Wood; 74cl AA/John Wood; 74cr Richard Moss; 74bl AA/John Wood; 74br AA/Richard Ireland; 75t AA/Rupert Tenison; 75c AA/Caroline Jones; 75b AA/Rupert Tenison; 77 AA/John Wood; 83 AA/John Wood; 86 AA/John Wood; 96 AA/John Wood; 98/99 AA/John Wood; 101t AA/Roger Moss; 101bl AA/John Wood; 101cr AA/John Wood; 101br AA/John Wood; 102cl AA/Caroline Jones; 102cr AA/Roger Moss; 102b AA/John Wood; 103t AA/John Wood; 103c AA/John Wood; 103b AA/John Wood; 105 AA/Roger Moss; 112 AA/John Wood; 117 AA/John Wood; 118 AA/John Wood; 122 AA/John Wood; 124/125 AA/Roger Moss; 127tl AA/Rupert Tenison; 127tr AA/John Wood; 127b AA/Roger Moss; 128cl AA/John Wood; 128cr AA/John Wood; 128b AA/John Wood; 129t AA/John Wood; 129b AA/Caroline Jones; 133 AA/Rupert Tenison; 143 AA/Adam Burton; 150 AA/John Wood.

Every effort has been made to trace the copyright holders, and we apologise in advance for any accidental errors. We would be happy to apply the corrections in the following edition of this publication.